Come to the Table

Food, Fellowship, and a Celebration of God's Bounty

"I will sing to the LORD, because He has dealt bountifully with me."
[Psalm 13:6]

Come to the Table

Food, Fellowship, and a Celebration of God's Bounty

Benita Long

Artistic & Floral Design Susan Wilson

Recipes & Food Styling Ann Mitchell

Photographs Sammy Anderson

Valediction by Steve Wingfield

THOMAS NELSON
Since 1798

NASHVILLE   DALLAS   MEXICO CITY   RIO DE JANEIRO   BEIJING

Published in Nashville, Tennessee, by Thomas Nelson. Thomas Nelson is a registered trademark of Thomas Nelson, Inc.

THE NEW KING JAMES VERSION. © 1982 by Thomas Nelson, Inc. Used by permission. All rights reserved.

Thomas Nelson, Inc., titles may be purchased in bulk for educational, business, fund-raising, or sales promotional use. For information, please e-mail SpecialMarkets@ThomasNelson.com.

Library of Congress Cataloging-in-Publication Data

Long, Benita, 1949–
          Come to the table : food and fellowship for celebrating God's bounty /
by Benita Long ; foreword by Steve Wingfield ; Sammy Anderson,
photographer ; Ann Mitchell, food editor ; Susan Wilson, executive designer.
          p. cm.
     Includes index.
     ISBN 978-1-4016-0385-4
     1. Cookery, American. I. Title.
     TX715.L8186 2008
     641.5973—dc22

2008012653

Printed in the United States
     11 12 TP 8

The Path of Celebration | Table of Contents

Our Friends Greet You
[3 John 14]

An Invitation, A Welcome, and A Challenge

Please, dear reader, join us at the table. We are ready and set to celebrate. We invite you to move through these pages, where celebration is presented as a living thankfulness. It is not confined to holidays, holy days, or even to days of special blessing. We are invited and called to celebrate, every day, the munificent, temporal gifts of God. Joyous living has the power to transform the journey of life into sacred travel, which, by definition is pilgrimage. Life as such in no way diminishes the traditional spiritual disciplines, but enhances them. To assist you in this process, we have a Path of Celebration, one that will "drip with abundance" [Psalm 65:11]. Its goal is to offer visual inspiration for a joy-filled life. The "paths they have not known" of Isaiah [42:16] belong to God's heaven. Our Path is of His earth. It celebrates the Lord's bountiful gift of daily nourishment. More than a gift, it was and is, a generous endowment. How we receive it and offer it to others is important to God. The appeal is universal, the possibilities immense. A voice from the fourth century, that of Gregory of Nyssa, tells us that "the sacred is everywhere." Look for something on every page. In addition to innovative ideas for preparing and serving food, our Path of Celebration includes thoughts and reflections for your spiritual nourishment. You may choose to simply peruse these pages, or you may decide to become an active participant. In A.D. 1106, the Russian Abbot Daniel made a pilgrimage to the Holy Land. Upon his return, he concluded that in many ways, reading about such travel was as beneficial as the journey itself. Our word for journey comes from the French *jour*, meaning day. We hope that in your own personal journey you will find the promised joy of each day, and that as for all true pilgrims, your path and your goal will merge.

"Whatever you can do, or dream you can, begin it."
[Johann Wolfgang Von Goethe, 1749–1832]

Throughout *Come To The Table, Food, Fellowship, and a Celebration of God's Bounty*, you will notice that very few people appear. This is our personal way of inviting you to claim each setting as your own. In like manner the beautiful plates are often pictured before any food is placed on them. This provides us all with a vivid reminder that more important than what is served is the grace with which it is prepared and offered. We are indeed the beneficiaries of God's promise of prosperity and peace, "That the mountains shall drip with new wine, The hills shall flow with milk, And all the brooks of Judah shall be flooded with water" [Joel 3:18]. Doesn't this just make you want to celebrate!

"I know that nothing is better for them than to rejoice, and to do good in their lives, and also that every man should eat and drink and enjoy the good of all his labor—it is the gift of God."
[Ecclesiastes 3:12]

It Is Pleasant for the Eyes to Behold the Sun

[Ecclesiastes 11:7]

The First Meal of the Day

How do you break the fast of night? Is the first nourishment of your day physical or is it spiritual? Are your earliest hours hurried and hectic or more leisurely? Whatever your routine, morning is a time for fresh sustenance from the earth, and for renewed thinking as well. The reflections in this section center around the nature of morning. Using the Bible as a "lens" [Marcus Borg], they shed new light on this beautiful time of day. What did God mean when He "called the light Day" [Genesis 1:5]?

Throughout the Bible, morning is imagined in many ways. In Genesis 3:8 it is the "cool" of day and in I Samuel 9:26 it is the "dawning." In more human imagery, Job 41:18 calls it the "eyelids" and Solomon describes it as the time that day "breathes." On his deathbed, King David prays for a king "like the light of the morning" [2 Samuel 23:4]. In the New Testament, Paul uses the image of morning as an opportunity for Christians to "put on the armor of light" [Romans 13:12].

In like manner, this imagery has often tethered poets to the Bible. We hope that you will enjoy hearing their combined voices. The pages of this section are to entice you! Receive your first meal of the day with gladness. Recall often the words of the poet Henry David Thoreau: "Renew thyself completely each day, do it again, and again, and forever again."

Yet the inward man is being renewed day by day.
[2 Corinthians 4:16]

Oh Lord, with each returning morn
Thine image to our hearts is born.
Oh may we ever clearly see
Our Savior and our God in Thee.
O joyful be the passing day
With thoughts as clear as morning's ray
With faith like noontide shining bright
Our souls unshadowed by the night.
[Ambrose of Milan, c. 340–397]

The First Meal of the Day

Father, we praise Thee,
now the night is over:
Active and watchful stand we all before thee:
Singing we offer prayer and meditation:
Thus we adore Thee.
[Gregory the Great, 540–604]

Italian Sausage Strata

Makes 6 to 8 servings

½	pound hot or mild Italian sausage, casings removed
4	tablespoons (½ stick) softened butter, divided
8	ounces sliced white or crimini mushrooms
6	slices whole wheat bread, crusts removed
12	ounces New York sharp Cheddar cheese, grated
4	eggs, beaten
2	cups whole milk
1	teaspoon dry mustard
	salt, to taste

Cook the sausage in 2 tablespoons of the butter, breaking the meat into small pieces. Remove the sausage from the pan and set aside. Add the mushrooms to the pan and sauté in the drippings. Butter one side of each bread slice with the remaining butter. In a 1½-quart round casserole, layer 3 slices of the bread, half of the sausage, half of the mushrooms, and half of the shredded cheese. Repeat the layers. Combine the eggs, milk, mustard, and salt. Pour over the layers and refrigerate for at least 2 hours or preferably overnight.

Preheat the oven to 325 degrees. Bake for 1 hour or until a knife inserted in the center comes out clean.

Jesus answered,
"Are there not twelve hours in the day?
If anyone walks in the day, he does not stumble, because he sees the light of this world."
[John 11:9]

"But let those who love Him be like the sun when it comes out in full strength."
[Judges 5:31]

Orange Cranberry Bread

Makes 2 loaves

1	navel orange (about ½ pound)
2¼	cups sugar, divided
3	cups fresh cranberries
4	eggs, lightly beaten
1¼	cups vegetable oil
3	cups all-purpose flour
1	tablespoon ground cinnamon
1	teaspoon baking soda
1	teaspoon salt
1	cup chopped pecans

Slice the unpeeled orange into small sections, removing any seeds and tough white membrane. In a food processor or blender, combine the orange slices and 1¼ cups of the sugar and pulse until the oranges are finely diced. Add the cranberries and pulse until the oranges and cranberries are very finely minced. Set aside for at least 30 minutes for the juices to form.

Preheat the oven to 350 degrees. Grease and flour two 9 x 5-inch loaf pans. In a medium mixing bowl, combine the cranberry mixture, eggs, and oil and mix well. In a large mixing bowl, combine the flour, the remaining 1 cup sugar, the cinnamon, baking soda, salt, and pecans. Add the cranberry mixture to the dry ingredients and stir gently until blended. Divide the batter evenly between each loaf pan. Bake for 45 to 55 minutes or until a toothpick inserted into the center comes out clean.

Note: This bread is delicious toasted.

✝

My voice you shall hear in the morning, O Lord,
In the morning I will direct it to you, and I will look up.
[Psalm 5:3]

Every morn shall lead thee through
Fresh baptisms of the dew.
[John Greenleaf Whittier, 1807–1892]

Parmesan Grits Casserole

Makes 8 to 10 servings

2½	cups water
4	cups milk
1¾	cups grits
1	clove garlic, crushed
12	tablespoons (1½ sticks) butter
3	eggs, beaten
1	cup Parmesan cheese, divided
1½	teaspoons salt
½	teaspoon black pepper
½	teaspoon white pepper
	paprika

Preheat the oven to 350 degrees. Bring the water and milk to a boil in a large saucepan over medium heat. Add the grits and cook until thick, stirring frequently. Add the garlic and butter and cool slightly. Add the eggs, ½ cup of the cheese, the salt, black pepper, and white pepper. Pour into a 2-quart baking dish. Top with the remaining ½ cup cheese and the paprika. Bake for 45 minutes or until set in the center.

I, Jesus . . . the Bright and Morning Star.
[Revelation 22:16]

Albert Einstein once wrote that religion without science is blind, and science without religion is lame. The parallels between the morning star of science and the Morning Star of faith would no doubt have bemused that great genius. The morning star of science rises at daybreak. Known as Sirius, it is the brightest star in the universe. When at its hottest point, rivers overflow and the land is renewed. Ancient people dated their years by its positioning. Slightly to the west of Sirius is a prophet star, Mirzan, possibly meaning "herald" in Arabic. This name was often given to other stars that preceded or heralded the rising of a brighter star. When Jesus called himself the Morning Star, he knew these things. He also knew that the present-day astronomers would remain perplexed as to why, over the centuries, Sirius had changed colors. For two thousand years it was described as red. In an observation in about 1000 B.C. a change was noted. Why? Jesus could easily have explained that it was His earthly ancestor David to whom God had first promised a Savior of royal blood. In 1000 B.C. David was King of Israel, and in that year coppery-colored Sirius changed to white!

Marian's Brunch Apricots

Makes 12 servings

4	(15-ounce) cans apricot halves
1	(15-ounce) can pitted sour cherries
1½	cups fresh or frozen blueberries
35	Ritz crackers, crushed
⅔	cup packed light brown sugar
8	tablespoons (1 stick) butter, melted

Preheat the oven to 325 degrees. In a 2-quart casserole layer one half of the apricots, cherries, and blueberries. Sprinkle with one half the cracker crumbs and brown sugar. Repeat layers. Pour the melted butter on top. Bake for 30 to 45 minutes, or until the mixture is hot and bubbly.

Very early in the morning.

[Mark 16:2]

For all Christians, the morning of mornings is when Mary Magdalene, Mary the mother of James, and Salome find the empty tomb of our Resurrected Lord. That God chose this time of day is not surprising. The Bible is filled with stories of early risers: Abimelech, Abraham, Jacob, Laban, Joseph, Moses, Balaam, Joshua, Gideon, Samuel, Saul, David, and, of course, Jesus with his disciples. The virtuous wife of Proverbs 31:15, who "rises while it is yet night, and provides food for her household" remains nameless! "Give her of the fruit of her hands, and let her own works praise her in the gates" [verse 31:31].

Creamed Chicken on Cornbread

Makes 6 to 8 servings

1½	pounds bone-in chicken breasts, poached
½	cup sliced green onions
1	cup chopped celery
8	ounces sliced mushrooms
8	tablespoons (1 stick) butter, divided
¼	cup flour
1½	cups milk or half-and-half
½	cup chicken broth
2	egg yolks, lightly beaten
½	cup green peas (if frozen, thawed)
2	hard-boiled eggs, sliced
	salt and pepper, to taste
6	to 8 pieces cornbread, split in half

Remove the chicken from the bone and cut into small pieces. Set aside.

Sauté the green onions, celery, and mushrooms in 4 tablespoons of the butter in a large saucepan until tender. Remove from the pan and set aside. Melt the remaining 4 tablespoons butter and stir in the flour until smooth. In a bowl combine the milk, broth, and egg yolks. Add to the flour and stir over low heat until thick and smooth. Stir in the sautéed vegetables, chicken, peas, and hard-boiled eggs. Season with salt and pepper. If necessary, stir in a small amount of broth or milk to thin. Serve hot over the halved cornbread slices.

Awake, lute
and harp
I will awaken the dawn.
[Psalm 108:2]

The innocent brightness of a newborn day
Is lovely yet.
[William Wordsworth, 1770–1850]

Tomato Gruyère Pie

Makes 6 to 8 servings

2	(9-inch) refrigerated pie dough rounds, unfolded and rolled together
4	medium ripe tomatoes, peeled, seeded, and sliced
1½	cups grated aged Gruyère cheese
1½	cups good quality mayonnaise
8	large fresh basil leaves, chopped
3	tablespoons chopped green onions
	pepper, to taste
	paprika, for color

Preheat the oven to 400 degrees. Place the pie crust into a 9-inch deep-dish pie pan. Bake the pie crust for 5 minutes.

Reduce the oven temperature to 350 degrees. Arrange the tomatoes in circles over the crust. In a bowl combine the cheese, mayonnaise, basil, green onions, and pepper. Spread over the tomatoes. Sprinkle with paprika. Bake for 30 to 40 minutes, or until bubbly.

If morning skies,
Books, and my food, and summer rain
Knocked on my sullen heart in vain –
Lord, thy most pointed pleasure take,
And stab my spirit broad awake.
[Robert Louis Stevenson, 1850–1894]

Glazed Lemon Muffins

Makes 72 mini muffins

muffins

3	cups all-purpose flour
2	cups granulated sugar
1½	teaspoons baking powder
1	teaspoon salt
1½	cups corn oil
1½	cups milk
3	eggs, slightly beaten
1	teaspoon lemon extract

glaze

2	medium oranges, zested and juiced
2	lemons, zested and juiced
1	pound confectioners' sugar, sifted

To make the muffins, preheat the oven to 350 degrees. Coat six 12-cup mini-muffin pans with nonstick cooking spray. In a large mixing bowl, sift together the flour, sugar, baking powder, and salt. In a medium mixing bowl, combine the oil, milk, eggs, and lemon extract and beat until smooth. Add the dry mixture to the wet ingredients and stir until just moist. Pour the batter into the muffin pans about three-quarters full. Bake for 10 to 12 minutes or until a toothpick comes out clean. Cool in the pans for a few minutes.

To prepare the glaze, combine the juices, zests, and confectioners' sugar. Mix well. Dip the warm muffins into the glaze and dry on wire racks set over waxed paper. These freeze beautifully!

Christ, whose
glory fills the skies
Christ, the true, the only light
Sun of Righteousness arise
Triumph o'er the shades of night;
Day-spring from on high be near
Day-star in my heart appear
[Charles Wesley, 1707–1788]

Spicy Hash Browns

Makes 4 servings

8	medium red potatoes
4	tablespoons (½ stick) butter
1	large mild onion, chopped
½	pound Andouille sausage, chopped into small cubes
	salt and pepper, to taste

In a medium saucepan cover the potatoes with water and simmer until done; drain. When cool enough to handle, slice the potatoes into ¼-inch rounds.

In a large skillet, melt the butter and cook the onion until golden. Add the potatoes and sausage to the pan and pat down evenly. Cook until brown on the bottom. Carefully turn over with a large spatula to keep the hash browns from breaking apart. Continue to cook until brown on the other side. Season with salt and pepper.

It is good to give thanks to the Lord.
And to sing praises to Your name, O Most High;
To declare Your loving kindness in the morning,
And Your faithfulness every night.
[Psalm 92:1–2]

Once more the Heavenly Power
Makes all things new.
[Alfred Lord Tennyson, 1809–1892]

"If I take the wings of morning,

And dwell in the uttermost parts of the sea,

Even there Your hand shall lead me,

And Your right hand shall hold me."

[Psalm 139:9-10]

I Heard Your Voice in the Garden

[Genesis 3:10]

Parties, Picnics, and Lunch in a Basket

Come now, please join us in the garden, your ancestral home! As you embrace a daily routine of celebration, let your heart become one of a pilgrim, a sacred life traveler. Be aware, however, that no pilgrimage would be complete without a few unexpected turns.

Throughout history, in many traditions of faith, the moment of revelation or epiphany has come against a backdrop of the natural world. How then can we experience this nature, more specifically, the garden, differently? We anticipate that after perusing this chapter you will see these spaces as consecrated and will eagerly make a commitment to take as many meals there as possible.

In both the Old and New Testaments, gardens served a myriad of functions. They were places where food was both grown [Genesis 2:9; Jeremiah 29:5; Amos 9:14] and eaten [Esther 1:5; Song of Solomon 2:4]. They provided quiet retreat [Esther 7:7] and a place for meeting friends [John 18:1]. They afforded physical protection [Song of Solomon 1:17] and cool relief from the heat of the day [Genesis 3:8]. In addition to these pragmatic functions, the garden was used by Old and New Testaments writers as a tool of imagery. In Genesis, it represented beauty perfected [2:9]; in Isaiah, joy and gladness [51:3]. For Jeremiah, the garden signified a commitment [29:5] and in Ezekiel, it symbolized restoration [36:35]. Yet none of these representations are as powerful or as important as the central role played by the garden as the setting for man's reconciliation with God. We were meant to live in a garden, specifically, Eden. Within that paradise, mankind separated himself from his Creator and was forced into exile. Yet at that very moment, a forgiving Lord clothed his children [Genesis 3:21] and began planning their redemption. How poignant it is to remember that it was to another garden, Gethsemane, that Christ retreated to wage, and ultimately win, the battle for all humanity. It was in this garden that Jesus surrendered to the will of our Father. Was it not totally appropriate that the earthly body of the Savior was laid to rest for three days in the new tomb of a third garden, that belonging to Joseph of Arimathea? We experience the garden, not only as a place of magnificent creation and constant renewal, but also as a source of divine resurrection and ultimate redemption. It is our hope that the following pages will, in some small way, enable you to hear the "voice in the garden."

Our Lord has written the promise of the resurrection
not in words alone, but in every leaf in springtime.
[Martin Luther, 1483–1546]

Parties, Picnics, and Lunch in a Basket

Earth, with her thousand voices,
praises God.
[Samuel Taylor Coleridge, 1772–1834]

Old-Fashioned Potato Salad

Makes 8 servings

4	medium white potatoes, peeled and halved
1	medium mild onion, chopped
2	to 3 celery stalks, diced
¼	to ⅓ cup sweet pickle relish
1½	to 2 cups good quality mayonnaise
1	heaping tablespoon yellow mustard
3	hard-cooked eggs, chopped
1	heaping tablespoon chopped pimento
	salt and pepper, to taste
	dash of sugar

Put the potatoes in a saucepan, cover with water, and bring to a boil over high heat. Cook until tender but not mushy, about 10 minutes. Drain and set aside to cool. In a large bowl combine the onion, celery, relish, mayonnaise, mustard, eggs, pimento, salt, pepper, and sugar. Cube the potatoes, add to the bowl, and mix well. Refrigerate for at least 3 hours to allow the flavors to blend. This is even better the next day.

Our blessed Savior chose the garden for his oratory . . .
where [the] fragrant flowers, trees and perennial plants [are] the most natural and instructive hieroglyphics of our expected resurrection and mortality.
[John Evelyn, 1620–1706]

Kind hearts are the gardens,
kind thoughts are the roots

Kind words are the flowers, kind deeds are the fruits.
Take care of your garden and keep out the weeds,
Fill it with sunshine, kind words, and kind deeds.

[Henry Wadsworth Longfellow, 1807–1882]

Minted Fruit

A colorful mixture of berries and melons makes a lovely presentation.
This is also a wonderful breakfast dish for company.

Makes 6 to 8 servings

1	cup water
2	tablespoons sugar
1	tablespoon fresh mint leaves
8	cups mixed fruit, cut into bite-size pieces

In a saucepan bring the water to a boil and stir in the sugar. Continue to boil, stirring constantly, until the sugar is dissolved. When dissolved, remove the pan from the heat and let cool. Pour the cooled mixture into a blender. Add the mint and pulse until the mint is finely chopped. Place the fruit in a medium serving bowl, pour the sugar mixture over the fruit, and refrigerate. Serve chilled.

Build houses and dwell in them;
plant gardens and eat their fruit.
[Jeremiah 29:5]

Delectable Deviled Eggs

You can use your imagination for assorted colorful toppings such as olive halves, pimento slices, caviar, or sliced grape tomatoes. These will be the hit of the picnic.

Makes 12 servings

1	dozen large eggs, hard cooked and peeled
1	heaping tablespoon sweet pickle relish
¼	cup mayonnaise
2	teaspoons yellow mustard
1	teaspoon minced onion
2	tablespoons Durkee's Famous Sauce
	salt and pepper, to taste

Halve the eggs. Gently remove the yolks with a teaspoon and place in a mixing bowl. Mash the yolks with a fork. Add the relish, mayonnaise, mustard, onion, Durkee's, salt, and pepper and mix well. Fill the egg halves with this mixture. Garnish with topping of your choice.

. . . a little old-fashioned garden
where the flowers come together to praise the Lord
and teach all who look upon them to do likewise.
[Celia Laighton Thaxter, *An Island Garden*, 1894]

Green Apple Cole Slaw

Makes 8 to 10 servings

dressing
1	cup good quality mayonnaise
¼	cup distilled white vinegar
⅓	cup sugar
	salt and pepper, to taste

cole slaw
1	medium green cabbage (about 1½ pounds), shredded
1	medium sweet onion, finely chopped
1	carrot, grated
2	tart green apples, chopped

For the dressing, combine the mayonnaise, vinegar, sugar, salt, and pepper in a small bowl. Mix well.

For the cole slaw, combine the cabbage, onion, carrot, and green apples in a medium serving bowl. Pour the dressing over the salad and refrigerate for several hours for the flavors to blend.

God is everywhere, it is true, and He that made all things
is not contained or confined to dwell in any place.
[St. Augustine Letter 78, 3]

Sun and light and brightness, the running waters of a perennial fountain, our own mind and language and spirit,
the sweet fragrance of a flowering rose, are images of the Holy and Eternal Trinity.
[St. John of Damascus, 675–749]

God's Garden

The Lord God planted a garden
In the first white days of the world,
And He set there an angel warden
In a garment of light unfurled.

So near to the peace of Heaven,
That the hawk might nest with the wren,
For there in the cool of the even
God walked with the first of men.

And I dream that these garden-closes
With their shade and their sun-flecked sod
And their lilies and bowers of roses,
Were laid by the hand of God.

The kiss of the sun for pardon,
The song of the birds for mirth,--
One is nearer God's heart in a garden
Than anywhere else on earth.

For He broke it for us in a garden
Under the olive-trees
Where the angel of strength was the warden
And the soul of the world found ease.

[Dorothy Frances Gurney. 1858–1932]

Peppermint Ice Cream

Makes 1 gallon

4	cups milk
2¼	cups sugar
1	teaspoon salt
1	cup half-and-half
4	cups whipping cream
1½	tablespoons peppermint extract
1	cup crushed hard peppermint candy

Bring the milk to a boil in a large saucepan. Remove from the heat and stir in the sugar and salt until dissolved. Stir in the half-and-half, whipping cream, and peppermint extract. Refrigerate for at least 30 minutes.

Prepare a 4-quart ice cream maker according to directions. Pour the chilled mixture into the ice cream can and churn until almost ready. Pour the peppermint candy into the ice cream and continue churning until ready. Remove the dasher from the can and freeze the ice cream for several hours to allow it to harden.

Grilled Lemon Chicken

Makes 6 servings

chicken

3	lemons
1½	cups extra-virgin olive oil
2	cloves garlic, minced
1	bay leaf
3	tablespoons chopped fresh basil (1 tablespoon dried)
1	teaspoon sea salt
	cracked pepper, to taste
6	bone-in chicken breasts, skinned

lemon sauce

1	tablespoon chopped fresh parsley (1 teaspoon dried)
2	tablespoons chopped fresh basil (2 teaspoons dried)
¼	cup fresh lemon juice
¼	cup red wine vinegar
2	tablespoons sugar
1	cup extra-virgin olive oil

For the chicken, grate the rind from one of the lemons; set aside. Squeeze the juice from all of the lemons into a large bowl. Add the grated lemon rind, olive oil, garlic, bay leaf, basil, salt, and pepper and mix well. Place the chicken in a zip-top plastic bag and pour the marinade over the chicken. Seal the bag and refrigerate for several hours or overnight. Remove the chicken from the bag and reserve the marinade. Preheat the grill to medium-high heat and grill the chicken breasts, turning several times and basting with the reserved marinade. Chill until ready to serve.

For the lemon sauce, combine the parsley, basil, lemon juice, vinegar, and sugar in a small bowl. Whisk in the olive oil until mixed well. Serve with the chilled grilled chicken.

A garden was the habitation of our first parents before the Fall.
It is naturally apt to fill the mind with calmness and tranquility and to lay all its turbulent passions at rest. It gives us great insight into the contrivance and wisdom of providence and suggests innumerable subjects for meditation. I cannot but think the very complacency and satisfaction which a man takes in these works of nature, to be laudable, if not a virtuous habit of mind.
[Joseph Addison, *The Spectator*, No. 477, 6 Sept. 1712]

Cream of Fennel Soup

Makes 8 servings

4	tablespoons (½ stick) butter
1	large sweet onion, about ¾ pound, thinly sliced
2	pounds fresh fennel bulbs, trimmed and thinly sliced
1	pound white potatoes, peeled and cubed
4	cups chicken stock
	juice of 1 lemon
1	teaspoon dried oregano
1	cup half-and-half
	salt and pepper, to taste

Melt the butter in a large saucepan over medium-high heat. Sauté the onion and fennel in the butter for about 10 minutes. Add the potatoes, chicken stock, and lemon juice to the pan. Simmer for about 45 minutes until the vegetables are very tender. Purée the soup in batches in a food processor or blender. Return the soup to the pan and add the oregano, half-and-half, salt, and pepper. This soup is delicious hot or cold.

He will make her wilderness like Eden,
And her desert like the garden of the Lord;
Joy and gladness will be found in it, Thanksgiving and the voice of melody.
[Isaiah 51:3]

Grilled Lamb Burgers

Nature's Season Salt is a mixture of garlic, pepper, and salt, among other seasonings.
It is different than orange salt like Lawry's and better with this recipe.

Makes 6 servings

3	large red onions, divided
¼	cup (½ stick) butter
	salt and pepper, to taste
2	pounds ground lamb
2	teaspoons chopped garlic
1	tablespoon chopped fresh rosemary
2	tablespoons chopped fresh mint
1	teaspoon Nature's Season Salt
6	whole wheat sandwich buns
	Dijon mustard
6	lettuce leaves

Chop half of 1 onion into small pieces and reserve to mix into the
burgers. Thinly slice the remaining 2½ onions. Melt the butter in
a skillet over medium-high heat. Add the onion slices, salt, and
pepper and sauté until soft. Set aside.

Preheat the grill until hot. Combine the lamb, the reserved chopped onion, the garlic, rosemary, mint, and
Nature's Season Salt. Shape into 6 patties. Cook the patties until the desired degree of doneness. Spread
the mustard on the buns and top each bun with a lamb burger, sautéed onions, and a lettuce leaf.

God Almighty first planted a garden;
and indeed, it is the purest of human pleasures.
[Francis Bacon, 1561–1626]

Those who contemplate the beauty of the earth find reserves of strength that will endure
as long as life lasts. There is something infinitely healing in the repeated refrains of nature,
the assurance that dawn comes after night, and spring after winter.
[Rachael Carson, 1907–1964]

Eat There and Rejoice Before the Lord Your God

[Deuteronomy 27:7]

Dinner on the Grounds

Catherine of Sienna (1347–1380) was one of twenty-five children who, at a very early age, committed her life to Christ. Because her activities were both social and ecclesiastical, her advice and counsel were sought by secular and religious leaders alike. Her writings were among the first to introduce the idea that Christians are travelers across the bridge from earth to heaven. She saw the Church as a hostelry, a stopping place, where such pilgrims could find refreshment. Congregational meals bear marvelous witness to this supposition. Partaking of meals in the House of the Lord is historically correct. It is a holy command. Deuteronomy 27 recounts the story of Moses and the elders obeying God's command to "eat there" after they established a place of worship [verse 7]. Upon placing the ark of the covenant in the tabernacle, David ate and distributed food to the Israelites, men and women alike; "a loaf of bread, a piece of meat, and a cake of raisins" [1 Chronicles 16:1-3]. A thousand years later, Jesus, in explaining the nature of the Sabbath, reminded his followers, "what David did when he was hungry, he and those who were with him: how he went into the house of God, took and ate the showbread, and also gave some to those with him" [Luke 6:3-4]. In His life on earth, Jesus thought that celebrations held at the Temple were important. Are we not privileged to continue such a tradition?

How lovely is Your tabernacle, O Lord of hosts!
My soul longs, yes, even faints for the courts of the Lord;
Blessed are those who dwell in Your house;
They will still be praising You.
[Psalm 84:1–2, 4]

Consider the word *host*. To some it signifies the heavenly band of angels that proclaimed the birth of our Savior. In Latin the word *hostis* means stranger or foreigner. Paul appropriately wrote the following words to the Ephesians, hoping that the early Christians would feel at home with God: "Now, therefore, you are no longer strangers and foreigners, but fellow citizens with the saints and members of the household of God" [2:19]. To others, the word *host* may call to mind the body of Christ, the bread of Communion. Oftentimes, when we think of a host today, we think of one who entertains guests in his own home at his own expense; a person who presides over any social gathering. Since all good gifts come from God, consider who may be the real host the next time you are invited to a congregational celebration.

Dinner on the Grounds

Bring life to our spirits and
A sense of joy to our living.
[James Kirk, *When We Gather*]

But those who have gathered it shall eat it,
And praise the Lord;
Those who have brought it together
shall drink it in My holy courts.
[Isaiah 62:9]

Ham and Linguini Casserole

Makes 10 to 12 servings

2	pounds asparagus, cut into thirds
⅓	cup butter
⅓	cup flour
2	cups half-and-half
1½	cups milk
⅓	cup chicken broth
¾	cup shredded sharp Cheddar cheese, divided
⅔	cup shredded Parmesan cheese, divided
2	tablespoons lemon juice
1	tablespoon grated onion
1	teaspoon dry mustard
1	tablespoon chopped fresh parsley
1½	teaspoons salt
	cracked pepper, to taste
4	cups cubed cooked ham
½	pound linguini, cooked and drained
	paprika for color

Preheat the oven to 350 degrees. Cook the asparagus in boiling salted water about 5 minutes or until just tender. Drain the asparagus and then plunge into a bowl of ice water to stop the cooking and hold the color. Drain and set aside.

In a 4-quart saucepan, melt the butter over medium heat. Add the flour and stir for 1 minute. Remove the pan from the heat and stir in the half-and-half, milk, and chicken broth until well blended. Return the pan to the heat and cook, stirring constantly, until thickened. Stir in ½ cup of the Cheddar cheese, ⅓ cup of the Parmesan cheese, the lemon juice, onion, dry mustard, parsley, salt, and pepper. In a large bowl, combine the ham and linguini. Pour the sauce over the linguini, tossing to mix.

In a 3-quart casserole, layer half the linguine mixture. Cover with the steamed asparagus and top with the remaining linguine mixture. Sprinkle with the remaining ¼ cup Cheddar cheese, ⅓ cup Parmesan cheese, and the paprika. Bake for about 45 minutes until bubbly and hot throughout. This dish freezes well.

Grilled Chicken Pasta Salad

Makes 12 to 14 servings

dressing

1	cup fresh basil leaves
1	clove garlic, minced
1	tablespoon Dijon mustard
¼	cup red wine vinegar
	juice of 1 lemon
⅔	cup extra-virgin olive oil
	salt and cracked pepper, to taste

salad

16	ounces rotini pasta, or other similar size pasta
4	boneless, skinless chicken breast halves
	lemon pepper, to taste
½	cup fresh or frozen cooked green peas
1	(14-ounce) can quartered artichoke hearts, drained
2	red bell peppers, roasted and cut into strips
4	scallions, chopped (both bottoms and tops with 2 inches green parts)
½	cup Niçoise olives, pitted
1	cup broccoli florets
	freshly grated Parmigiano-Reggiano cheese

For the dressing, combine the basil, garlic, mustard, vinegar, and lemon juice in a food processor. Pulse until the basil is chopped. Add the oil slowly while pulsing. Season with salt and pepper.

For the salad, cook the pasta until al dente. Drain and set aside to cool.

Heat a grill to medium. Sprinkle the chicken with lemon pepper and grill until the chicken is done. When cool enough to handle, slice into strips.

In a serving bowl combine the chicken, pasta, peas, artichoke hearts, bell peppers, scallions, olives, and broccoli. Toss with the dressing. Chill for at least 3 hours. Top with Parmigiano-Reggiano cheese.

Sunshine Salad

Makes 20 servings

dressing

1	cup corn oil
½	cup cider vinegar
¼	cup sugar
1	tablespoon poppy seeds
1	teaspoon dry mustard
1	teaspoon sea salt
	pepper, to taste

salad

1	pound soft salad greens
1	pound baby spinach
2	kiwis, peeled and sliced
1	European cucumber, sliced
1	pint grape tomatoes, halved
8	ounces sliced fresh mushrooms
1	(14-ounce) can mandarin oranges, drained
1	pint fresh strawberries, hulled and sliced
1	bunch spring onions, chopped

For the dressing, in a bowl whisk together the oil, vinegar, sugar, poppy seeds, dry mustard, salt, and pepper. Refrigerate until ready to use.

For the salad, in a large serving bowl gently toss the salad greens, spinach, kiwis, cucumber, tomatoes, mushrooms, mandarin oranges, strawberries, and spring onions. Just before servings, add the dressing and toss.

Note: This salad is beautiful and delicious. In the summer any fresh fruit may be substituted. Blackberries, blueberries, raspberries, and fresh peaches also make a lovely presentation.

And let the beauty of the Lord our God be upon us,
and establish the work of our hands for us; yes, establish the work of our hands.
[Psalm 90:17]

Green Beans with Toasted Pine Nuts

Nature's Season Salt is a mixture of garlic, pepper, and salt, among other seasonings. It is different than orange salt like Lawry's and better with this recipe.

Makes 8 servings

1½	pounds haricots verts or small tender green beans, trimmed
¼	cup pine nuts, toasted
1½	teaspoons finely grated fresh lemon zest
4	teaspoons extra-virgin olive oil

Cook the beans in boiling salted water until tender. Plunge in ice water and drain. Refrigerate until ready to serve.

Just before serving reheat the beans in the microwave until warm. Place in a 2-quart casserole. Toss with the pine nuts, lemon zest, olive oil, and season salt. Serve warm or at room temperature.

An Opportunity to Serve

Sing to the Lord with cheerful voice;
Him serve with mirth.
[William Kethe, 1561]

These words of the beloved hymn based on Psalm 100, "All People That on Earth Do Dwell," can easily be viewed as inspiration to fulfill obligations of a social nature. The song continues to urge us to approach God's House with joy, ever mindful that it is He who feeds us. If your life is one blessed with extensive social opportunities, why not view church gatherings as occasions for giving rather than for receiving? The beautiful Puritan meditation in the Table Prayers section of this book thanks God for the privilege of "spreading happiness around." The angel at the tomb of Jesus said, "Go and tell" [Matthew 28:7]. When we share our time, with heartfelt gladness, are we not "telling" the story?

And from morn to set of sun,
Through the church the song goes on.
[Ignaz Franz, 1774]

All are needed by each one,

Nothing is fair or good alone.

[Ralph Waldo Emerson 1803-1882]

Gazpacho Aspic

Makes 8 servings

4	cups V-8 juice
1	tablespoon brown sugar
3	envelopes unflavored gelatin
¼	cup cold water
	splash of Tabasco sauce
3	tablespoons lemon juice
2	cloves garlic, minced
¾	cup chopped celery
¾	cup chopped cucumber
½	cup chopped yellow bell pepper
¼	cup chopped green onions
¼	cup chopped fresh parsley

In a medium saucepan over medium heat, combine the V-8 juice and brown sugar. Simmer for about 5 minutes. Soften the gelatin in the cold water for about 1 minute. Add the gelatin mixture to the hot V-8 mixture. Stir in the Tabasco sauce, lemon juice, and garlic. Refrigerate until slightly thick and stir in the celery, cucumber, bell pepper, onions, and parsley. Pour into an 8-cup ring mold and chill for several hours until set.

Hilaire Belloc was a moving force in the Christian literary revival of the early 20th century. In his 1902 classic, *Path to Rome*, he developed the idea that through association with like-minded people of faith, Christians could acquire an intellectual energy necessary for a life's work. "That now the manifold wisdom of God might be made known by the church" [Ephesians 3:10] was the work to which he alluded. Christians sharing food in God's living abode "energize" each other and the congregation as a whole, both physically and spiritually. It is ironic that Belloc, best known for his inspirational writing, was also famous for his great dinner parties!

"We who work for God should be lighthearted"
[St. Leonard of Port Maurice]

Cheddar Squash Strata

Makes 6 to 8 servings

4	tablespoons (½ stick) butter
3	pounds yellow squash, sliced
½	medium onion, chopped
2	eggs
½	cup milk
1	tablespoon light brown sugar
1	teaspoon salt
1	teaspoon ground sage, or
	1 tablespoon chopped fresh sage
2½	cups whole wheat bread cubes, crust removed
1	cup grated sharp Cheddar cheese, divided

In a large saucepan melt the butter over medium heat. Sauté the squash and onion until tender, about 12 minutes. Mash the squash with a fork.

Preheat the oven to 350 degrees. In a medium bowl beat the eggs. Add the milk, brown sugar, salt, and sage and mix. Add to the squash and onion mixture. In a 2-quart casserole layer half the bread, half the squash mixture, and ½ cup of the cheese. Repeat the layers, ending with the remaining ½ cup cheese. Bake for 45 minutes.

A Biblical Tradition, A Holy Command

*You shall eat before the Lord your God,
in the place where He chooses to
make His name abide.*
[Deuteronomy 14:23]

Grilled Asparagus with Blue Cheese

Makes 6 to 8 servings

30	medium asparagus spears, trimmed
½	pint grape tomatoes, halved
½	cup extra-virgin olive oil, divided
¼	cup chopped fresh chives
½	cup crumbled blue cheese
4	teaspoons red wine vinegar
	salt and pepper, to taste

Roast or grill the asparagus until tender. Place in a rectangular casserole. Put the tomatoes on a baking sheet and brush with about ¼ cup of the olive oil. Broil under high heat until the skins blister. Arrange the tomatoes on top of the asparagus. Sprinkle with the chives and blue cheese. Whisk the remaining ¼ cup of the oil and the vinegar together in a bowl until emulsified. Pour the mixture over the vegetables and season with salt and pepper.

A Place for Healing

"For first of all, when you come together as a church, I hear that there are divisions among you" [1 Corinthians 11:18]. After writing these words, Paul goes on to admonish church members who receive the Lord's Supper in a state of animosity. He advises them to stay at home. "What! Do you not have houses to eat and drink in?" [verse 22]. Could he not be writing to any of today's fractionalized congregations? Just as Olympic athletes used their games to enjoy a period of peace, congregations, in times of discouragement, can benefit from social gatherings. Differences of opinion will diminish, as God's people celebrate their common blessings.

"Let them bring me to Your holy hill and to Your tabernacle."
[Psalm 43:3]

Chunky Chocolate Hazelnut Cookies

Makes 48 cookies

16	tablespoons (2 sticks) butter, softened
1¼	cups brown sugar
2	large eggs
2¼	cups flour
¾	teaspoon baking soda
1	teaspoon salt
8	ounces white chocolate bits
8	ounces dark chocolate bits
1	cup hazelnuts

Preheat the oven to 350 degrees. In a large mixing bowl beat the butter and brown sugar together. Beat in the eggs. Mix the flour, baking soda, and salt together in a separate bowl. Gradually stir the dry mixture into the wet ingredients. Mix well. Stir in the chocolate bits and hazelnuts. Drop by tablespoons, about 2 inches apart, onto an ungreased cookie sheet. Bake for about 10 minutes.

A Promise of Favor

At the conclusion of a party, children eagerly anticipate being given a small treat or "favor," which in its original context was a token of love. Gathering in the House of God, in the name of His Son, for the purpose of sharing His gift of nourishment, positions us to actively experience God's favor. This feeling of sustenance and vitality is expressed in 1 Timothy 3:15, *"the house of God, which is the church of the living God, the pillar and ground of the truth."* It was no accident that it was at a meal, His last, that Christ revealed, *"I am the. . . truth. No one comes to the Father except through Me"* [John 14:6]. Meals and refreshments enjoyed together in a sanctified setting foreshadow God's ultimate favor or gift, *"that you may eat and drink at My table in My kingdom"* [Luke 22:30].

Spicy Apple Cake with Caramel Icing

Makes 8 to 12 servings

cake

1	cup corn oil
3	eggs, well beaten
2	cups sugar
1	teaspoon vanilla extract
3	cups cake flour
2	teaspoons baking powder
1	teaspoon baking soda
2	teaspoons pumpkin pie spice
1	teaspoon salt
1	cup chopped pecans
3	cups peeled and grated crisp apples, such as Granny Smith

caramel icing

3	cups firmly packed light brown sugar
12	tablespoons (1½ sticks) butter
⅛	teaspoon salt
¾	cup heavy cream
1	teaspoon vanilla extract

For the cake, preheat the oven to 350 degrees. Grease and flour a 13 x 9-inch baking pan. In a large mixing bowl beat the oil, eggs, and sugar until well mixed. Stir in the vanilla. Sift together the flour, baking powder, baking soda, pumpkin pie spice, and salt. Add to the wet ingredients and mix well. Add the pecans and apples and stir to combine. Spread the batter into the prepared pan and bake for 40 to 45 minutes, or until a toothpick inserted into the center comes out clean. Let the cake cool.

For the icing, combine the brown sugar, butter, salt, and cream in a heavy saucepan over low heat. Increase the heat and bring the mixture to a boil. Continue boiling until the mixture reaches the soft-ball stage on a candy thermometer (238 degrees), stirring often. Remove from the heat and cool to 110 degrees. Add the vanilla and beat with a wooden spoon until thick and creamy. Spread the icing over the cooled cake.

"Sustain me with cakes of raisins, refresh me with apples."
[Song of Solomon 2:5]

House to House, They Ate Their Food with Gladness

[Acts 2:46]

Four Small Group Dinners

The love that was exemplified in the Old Testament was perfected and personified in Christ. In Greek there are several words for love, one of them meaning "brotherly love." That word, *philos*, should be at the heart of every Christian gathering. Where better to practice this love than in the intimacy of a small group sharing a meal? Throughout history, such occasions have been a source of great social, as well as spiritual, transformation. Until the third century A.D., church buildings did not exist, so faith in Jesus Christ was continued by those who met and celebrated in their homes. Many years later, John Wesley reinstated these meetings, centered around the love feast. In more recent times, believers in Eastern Europe, under the yoke of Communism, practiced their faith in the milieu of small groups gathering for meals. To assemble for religious or political reasons was dangerous, so the sharing of food, ostensibly, gave these meetings a social nature. As serious as this all sounds, small group dinners were and are not only a source of great pleasure, but are integral to and consistent with our faith. So many religious traditions spurn happiness. God has created us so that we are predisposed to live a life of celebration. The very nature of our faith also encourages us to live in community with one another. Another final blessing is that, "There is nothing that enters a man from outside which can defile him" [Mark 7:15]. We have no forbidden foods!

Go, eat your bread with joy.
[Ecclesiastes 9:7]

Four Small Group Dinners

Stuffed Pork Tenderloin
with Spicy Cranberry Sauce | 88
Grilled Pineapple | 91
Spinach Parmigiana | 91

Flank Steak with Mushrooms | 92
New Potato and Sweet Onion Gratin | 95
Fresh Pear Salad | 96

Company Meat Loaf | 101
Grapefruit and Avocado Salad | 102
Potato Croquettes | 105

Lamb Kabobs | 106
Cremini Mushroom Orzo | 107
Santorini Salad | 109

Be kindly affectionate to one another . . .
given to hospitality.
[Romans 12:10, 13]

Stuffed Pork Tenderloin with Spicy Cranberry Sauce

Makes 4 to 6 servings

pork tenderloin

2	(1-pound) pork tenderloins
1	tablespoon minced garlic
1	tablespoon grated fresh ginger
1	(8-ounce) can diced pineapple, drained, reserving juice
2	teaspoons soy sauce
1	teaspoon ground cinnamon
4	thin slices prosciutto
¼	cup dried cranberries
2	tablespoons vegetable oil
	all-purpose flour for browning

sauce

1	(20-ounce) can pineapple slices, drained, reserving juice
1	(16-ounce) can whole-berry cranberry sauce
1	tablespoon soy sauce
3	tablespoons rice wine vinegar
½	teaspoon cinnamon
	red pepper flakes, to taste

For the pork, with a sharp knife cut each tenderloin lengthwise almost through. Lay each tenderloin flat between waxed paper and pound until ½ inch thick. Arrange the tenderloins in a baking dish. Place half the garlic and half the ginger on top of each tenderloin. Combine the reserved pineapple juice, soy sauce, and cinnamon and pour over the meat. Refrigerate the tenderloins for several hours or overnight.

Place 2 slices of prosciutto lengthwise on each pork tenderloin. Spoon half the diced pineapple and half the dried cranberries down the middle of each tenderloin. Roll the meat and fasten with kitchen twine. Turn the pork seam side down. Preheat the oven to 350 degrees. Heat the vegetable oil in a large skillet. Sprinkle the meat with flour and brown on all sides. Place the tenderloins in a roasting pan and roast until a meat thermometer inserted into the center of the pork registers 150 degrees, up to 30 minutes. Let rest 10 minutes. Remove the twine and slice into ½-inch pieces.

For the sauce, in a saucepan over medium heat, combine the reserved pineapple juice, cranberry sauce, soy sauce, vinegar, cinnamon, and red pepper flakes. Simmer the sauce for 10 minutes. Spoon the sauce over the pork and garnish with grilled pineapple slices (see page 91).

Note: Sweet and spicy! May be assembled ahead and cooked just before serving.

Grilled Pineapple

Makes 4 to 6 servings

	reserved pineapple slices from pork tenderloin (see page 88)
¼	cup firmly packed brown sugar
1	rounded teaspoon ground cinnamon

Preheat the oven to broil. Place the reserved pineapple slices on a broiler pan. Broil until the pineapple begins to brown. Remove from oven, turn slices over and sprinkle with a little sugar and cinnamon. Broil this side until brown and the sugar is caramelized. Serve as a garnish to the stuffed pork tenderloin. The pineapple may be grilled.

Spinach Parmigiana

Makes 4 to 6 servings

1	tablespoon butter
¾	cup chopped sweet onion, such as Vidalia
10	ounces baby spinach, coarsely chopped
1	tablespoon water
2	large eggs, lightly beaten
1	cup milk
1	cup grated Parmigiano-Reggiano cheese, divided
½	teaspoon salt
¼	teaspoon pepper
⅛	teaspoon ground nutmeg

Preheat the oven to 350 degrees. Melt the butter in a large skillet over medium-high heat and sauté the onion until tender. Add the spinach and water and cook until just wilted. Drain in a large sieve, pressing with a wooden spoon until all the liquid is drained. In a bowl whisk together the eggs, milk, ¾ cup of the cheese, the salt, pepper, and nutmeg. Stir into the spinach mixture. Pour into a lightly greased 1½-quart baking dish. Sprinkle with the remaining ¼ cup cheese and bake, uncovered, about 30 minutes, or until set in the center. Serve warm or at room temperature.

Flank Steak with Mushrooms

Makes 10-12 servings

steak

½	cup chopped shallots
1	cup teriyaki sauce
¼	cup orange juice
1	teaspoon crushed red pepper flakes
4	pounds flank steak

sauce

8	tablespoons (1 stick) butter
½	cup chopped shallots
24	ounces cremini mushrooms
8	ounces white mushrooms
½	cup balsamic vinegar
¼	cup soy sauce
¼	cup sugar

For the steak, combine the shallots, teriyaki sauce, orange juice, and red pepper flakes in a large shallow dish. Add the steak and marinate for up to 2 days in the refrigerator, turning occasionally.

For the sauce, melt the butter in a saucepan. Sauté the shallots in the butter until translucent. Add the mushrooms and sauté until the liquid is evaporated. In a small bowl mix the vinegar, soy sauce, and sugar together. Add to the mushrooms. Cook until slightly reduced.

Preheat the grill to medium. Grill the steak until medium rare. Let rest for a few minutes and slice diagonally across the grain. Serve the steak with the mushroom sauce.

All gifts are from God. Saying or writing "thank you" should be a great pleasure. Think of all the notes Paul wrote! Gaius, Publius, Lydia, Jason, Mnason, Priscilla, Aquila, and the natives at Malta are but some of the many to whom he extended personal notes of gratitude for their hospitality. Be ever mindful that many did so at great personal risk.

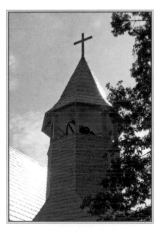

New Potato and Sweet Onion Gratin

Nature's Season Salt is a mixture of garlic, pepper, and salt, among other seasonings.
It is different than orange salt like Lawry's and better with this recipe.

Makes 12 servings

2	pounds red new potatoes (about 6 cups sliced)
2	pounds sweet onions (about 6 cups sliced)
8	tablespoons (1 stick) butter, cut into small pieces
	Nature's Season Salt
2	cups shredded Swiss cheese

Preheat the oven to 350 degrees. Thinly slice the potatoes using a food processor or by hand; set aside. Thinly slice the onions using a food processor or by hand. In a lightly greased 3-quart casserole, layer half the potatoes, half the onions, and dot with half the butter. Sprinkle with season salt. Repeat the layers and top with the Swiss cheese. Cover and bake for 30 minutes. Uncover and bake about 30 more minutes or until browned and bubbly. Test the center of the casserole with a sharp knife to be sure the potatoes are tender.

Rules of Etiquette

Jesus of Nazareth never refused an invitation to dinner! He visited humble abodes and attended great banquets, such as the one held in the house of Levi. In so doing, he left for us some very specific rules to follow when entertaining. As a guest, Jesus preferred the behavior of Mary who spent time with him, listening to him. Martha, who remained preoccupied with the preparations, was chastised.

In Mark 7, Jesus cautioned that, *"pitchers and cups . . . traditions of men"* should not be of greater importance than the heart of the one who serves. As beautiful as these things are, we must always remember that they are secondary. In Luke 19, Jesus commands Zacchaeus, the tax collector, sitting in a tree to, *". . . make haste and come down, for today I must stay at your house."* These few words are fraught with additional advice about extending hospitality. Jesus did not suggest going to an inn or public eating establishment, which, though limited in those days, did exist. He specified "your house." He also said "today," which reminds us that we do not always have much time to prepare. In many cultures of the world, preparation is an important component of celebration. If time is limited, ask your guests to participate. We should always remember and strive to emulate Zacchaeus who, *". . . made haste and came down, and received Him joyfully"* [Luke 19:6].

Fresh Pear Salad

Makes 6 to 8 servings

dressing

1	teaspoon dry mustard
½	teaspoon salt
	pepper, to taste
1	tablespoon honey
3	tablespoons cider vinegar
⅓	cup extra-virgin olive oil

salad

3	ripe pears, peeled and thinly sliced
1	Haas avocado, peeled and sliced
½	cup orange juice
6	cups baby lettuce or baby spinach
5	ounces Roquefort cheese
½	cup chopped green onions
½	cup caramelized pecans

For the dressing, combine the dry mustard, salt, pepper, honey, and vinegar in a bowl. Whisk in the olive oil to blend. Set aside.

For the salad, in a bowl toss the pears and avocado with the orange juice. Place the lettuce in a bowl and top with the pears and avocado mixture, the cheese, green onions, and pecans. Toss with the dressing just before serving.

Be hospitable to one another without grumbling.
As each one has received a gift, minister it to one another,
as good stewards of the manifold grace of God. [1 Peter 4:9–10]

And when we had come to Jerusalem, the brethren received us gladly.[Acts 21:17]

Company Meat Loaf

This is a very moist meat loaf that makes wonderful sandwiches on buns.

Makes 6 to 8 servings

meat loaf

2	eggs, beaten
1	(8-ounce) can tomato sauce
½	teaspoon dried thyme
½	teaspoon dried marjoram
1	teaspoon salt
	pepper, to taste
¼	to ½ cup chopped mild onion (Vidalia)
1½	pounds ground chuck
½	cup medium saltine cracker crumbs
½	cup chopped green bell pepper

sauce

1	(8-ounce) can tomato sauce
2	tablespoons light brown sugar
½	teaspoon Lawry's Seasoned Salt
1	tablespoon red wine vinegar
¼	teaspoon dried thyme
¼	teaspoon dried marjoram
	dash pepper

For the meat loaf, preheat the oven to 350 degrees. In a medium bowl, combine the eggs, tomato sauce, thyme, marjoram, salt, and pepper. Add the onion, ground chuck, cracker crumbs, and bell pepper and mix well. Shape the mixture into a loaf and place on a rimmed baking pan.

For the sauce, combine the tomato sauce, brown sugar, seasoned salt, vinegar, thyme, marjoram, and pepper. Pour the sauce over the meat loaf. Bake for about 1¼ hours. Pour off the excess juice.

If you have judged me to be faithful to the Lord, come to my house. . . .
[Acts 16:15]

Grapefruit and Avocado Salad

Makes 8 to 10 servings

salad

3	ruby red grapefruits
2	ripe avocados
12	ounces baby spinach
5	ounces fresh raspberries
3½	ounces honey-roasted almond slices

dressing

½	teaspoon powdered dry mustard
½	teaspoon salt
½	cup honey
3	tablespoons grapefruit juice
¼	cup raspberry balsamic vinegar
1	cup corn oil

To make the salad, peel and section the grapefruits, reserving 3 tablespoons of the juice for the dressing. Peel and slice the avocados into thin slices. In a salad bowl, place the spinach, sectioned grapefruit, sliced avocados, raspberries, and almonds.

To make the dressing, in a small bowl, mix the dry mustard and salt. Add the honey, grapefruit juice, and vinegar. Slowly add the corn oil, whisking until well blended. Toss with the salad and serve immediately.

"My son, eat honey because it is good,
and the honeycomb which is sweet to your taste; so shall the knowledge of wisdom be to your soul."
[Psalm 24:13-14]

"I am the rose of Sharon, and the lily of the valleys."
[Song of Solomon 2:1]

Potato Croquettes

Makes 4 to 6 servings

2	pounds russet potatoes, unpeeled
1	egg, beaten
¼	cup crumbled blue cheese
4	small green onions, sliced thinly
1	teaspoon salt
¼	teaspoon white pepper
1	cup crushed buttery cracker crumbs (about 20 crackers)
2	tablespoons butter
½	cup corn oil

Preheat the oven to 400 degrees. Bake the potatoes for about 1 hour or until tender. Slice the potatoes in half and let cool. Scoop out the potato into small bowl. Add the egg, blue cheese, green onions, salt, and pepper and mix lightly. Shape the potato mixture into 4 to 6 patties. Put the cracker crumbs onto a cutting board or plate and press each patty into the crumbs, making sure they stick and turning to coat both sides. Line a jelly-roll pan with waxed paper. Place the coated patties onto the prepared pan, cover, and refrigerate for up to 24 hours.

When ready to make the croquettes, remove them from the refrigerator and let come to room temperature. In a large nonstick pan, melt the butter and oil over medium-high heat. When hot, gently place the potato patties into the oil at least one inch apart. Cook both sides until golden brown, about 3 minutes per side. Serve immediately.

The Meal That Makes Us Family and Friends.

"We all need to eat and drink to stay alive. But having a meal is more than eating and drinking. It is celebrating the gifts of life we share. A meal together is one of the most intimate and sacred human events. Around the table we become vulnerable, filling one another's plates and cups and encouraging one another to eat and drink. Much more happens at a meal than satisfying hunger and quenching thirst. Around the table we become family, friends, community, yes, a body. "That is why it is so important to 'set' the table. Flowers, candles, colorful napkins all help us to say to one another, 'This is a very special time for us, let's enjoy it!'"

[Henri Nouwen, 1932–1996]

From Bread for the Journey: A Daybook of Wisdom and Faith by Henri J.M. Nouwen.

Copyright (c) 1997 by Henri J.M. Nouwen. Reprinted by permission of Harper Collins Publishers.

Lamb Kabobs

Makes 6 servings

¼	cup soy sauce
	juice of 1 lemon
½	cup extra-virgin olive oil
2	sprigs rosemary
4	cloves garlic, minced
	pepper, to taste
2	pounds top loin lamb, trimmed well and cut into 1½-inch cubes
1	red bell pepper, cut into chunks
1	yellow bell pepper, cut into chunks
2	medium red onions, peeled and cut into chunks
8	ounces small whole cremini mushrooms

Combine the soy sauce and lemon juice in a bowl. Stir in the olive oil, rosemary, garlic, and pepper to make a marinade. Combine the marinade and meat in a zip-top bag and refrigerate for several hours or overnight.

Preheat the grill. Drain the meat, reserving the marinade. Thread the meat, bell peppers, onions, and mushrooms onto 6 skewers. Cook, uncovered, basting frequently with the reserved marinade and turning several times until the meat is to the desired degree of doneness.

Cremini Mushroom Orzo

Makes 6 servings

2	cups chicken broth
1	cup orzo
1	tablespoon olive oil
⅓	cup chopped green onions
2	small zucchini, chopped
¼	cup chopped red bell pepper
8	ounces sliced cremini mushrooms
	salt and pepper, to taste
	Nature's Season Salt
½	cup Parmigiano-Reggiano cheese

Bring the chicken broth to a boil in a medium saucepan. Stir the orzo into the broth and cook until al dente. Drain. Add the olive oil to a skillet over medium-high heat. Add the green onions, zucchini, bell pepper, and mushrooms and sauté until tender, about 10 minutes. Combine the orzo and sautéed vegetables in a serving bowl. Season with salt, pepper, and season salt. Sprinkle with the Parmigiano-Reggiano cheese. May be served hot or at room temperature.

Santorini Salad

Makes 6 servings

dressing

¼	cup red wine vinegar
2	teaspoons lemon juice
2	cloves garlic, minced
1	heaping teaspoon dried oregano
1	teaspoon sea salt
	pepper, to taste
½	cup extra-virgin olive oil

salad

2	large tomatoes, seeded and cut into chunks
1	English cucumber, cut into chunks
1	cup pitted Kalamata olives
¼	to ½ cup thinly sliced red onion
5	ounces crumbled feta cheese

For the dressing, combine the vinegar, lemon juice, garlic, oregano, salt, and pepper in a small bowl. Whisk in the oil. Set aside.

For the salad, in a salad bowl combine the tomatoes, cucumber, olives, onion, and feta cheese. Toss with the dressing and refrigerate. Make ahead several hours for the flavors to blend.

Your Joy Will Be God's Missionary

Charles Spurgeon, born in 1834, was one of England's most popular clergymen.
Reflecting upon the words of Nehemiah, he wrote the following:

"Send out the heat of piety into your house and let all the neighbors participate in the blessing. . .
The joy of the Lord shall be observed throughout our neighborhood, and many who might otherwise have
been careless of true religion will then enquire, 'what makes these people glad, and creates such happy households?'
Your joy shall thus be God's missionary."

Why not let this thought inspire your small group to periodically invite guests?
"For God had made them rejoice . . . that the joy of Jerusalem was heard afar off."
[Nehemiah 12:43]

"Good food ends with good talk."
[G. K. Chesterton, 1874–1936]

Joy and Gladness, a Feast and a Holiday

Family Gatherings

Festive occasions are a time for us to bind New Testament love with the generous hospitality established in the Old Testament. The sons of Job took turns entertaining their entire family, which, in addition to the seven brothers, included three sisters [1:4-5]. Nehemiah proclaimed that, "At my table were one hundred and fifty" [5:17]. And remember Gaius Titius Justus, who hosted not only Paul but the whole church as well [Romans 16:23]!

Great family gatherings are truly "investments," which is actually a military term meaning "full siege." No one knew this better than a nineteenth-century Englishwoman by the name of Isabella Beeton. The wife of a publisher, she wrote a widely circulated book on household management. In it she stated, "As with the commander of an army . . . so it is with the mistress of a house." Maintaining our joy in the midst of extensive preparations can be a challenge for anyone. We hope that the visual and inspirational nourishment offered in this section will facilitate this, as you prepare for those special times. Nevertheless, the return on the expenditures of time, energy, and resources is put away in the memory bank of all those present. The gift of saying "remember when" is dependent upon what is done "now." It may also be helpful to you to reflect upon the words of Leo Tolstoy's character in *Resurrection*, Prince Nekhlyudov, who said, "Let everyone be himself and we'll all be as one." Is this not the sentiment of Proverbs 17:1, "Better is a dry morsel with quietness, than a house full of feasting with strife"? This was certainly the sentiment of Paul, as he consistently taught sensitivity to the habits of others. And on a much lighter side, think of all the marvelous leftovers! Calvin Trillin once said, "The most remarkable thing about my mother is that for thirty years she served nothing but leftovers. The original meal has never been found." A concluding thought comes from the first-century A.D. Roman philosopher, Epictetus: "Bear in mind that you should conduct yourself in life as at a feast." What could that mean for us? On days of special blessing, we are especially commanded:

"When you have eaten and are full, and have built beautiful houses and dwell in them . . .
you shall remember the Lord your God, for it is He who gives you power to get wealth,
that He may establish His covenant which He swore to your fathers, as it is this day."
[Deuteronomy 8:12, 18]

Family Gatherings

He brought me to the banqueting house,
And his banner over me was love.
[Song of Solomon 2:4]

Beef Tenderloin

Makes 10 servings

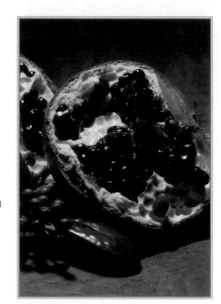

¼	cup Lawry's Seasoned Salt
2	tablespoons soy sauce
2	tablespoons lemon pepper
6	pounds beef tenderloin, trimmed

In a small bowl make a paste of the seasoned salt, soy sauce, and lemon pepper. Rub the paste over the tenderloin, coating all sides. Let sit at room temperature for 1 hour.

Preheat the broiler. Place the meat on a rack in the broiler pan and broil until golden brown, about 8 minutes. Turn the meat over and broil until the other side is golden brown, about 8 minutes. Remove the meat from the oven and reduce the oven temperature to 350 degrees. Sprinkle the meat with a little more soy sauce and seasoned salt and insert a meat thermometer into the thickest part. Roast the meat until the thermometer registers 120 degrees for medium rare. Let set for 10 minutes before carving.

"The soul of one who serves God always swims in joy,
always keeps holiday, and is always in a mood for singing."
[St. John of the Cross]

Those who possess the spirit of God through faith are granted "spiritual fruit," the first being love, the second joy. [Galatians 5:22]. This is particularly evident on those days throughout the Christian year that are characterized by great feasting. The visual and spiritual nourishment offered in this section will facilitate your preparations for such occasions. "You shall eat in plenty and be satisfied, and praise the name of the Lord your God, who has dealt wondrously with you" [Joel 2:26].

Wild Rice with Mushrooms

Makes 6 to 8 servings

4	tablespoons (½ stick) butter
½	cup chopped shallots
8	ounces sliced mushrooms
½	red bell pepper, chopped
½	cup sliced almonds
6	ounces wild rice, rinsed and drained
3	cups chicken broth

Preheat the oven to 325 degrees. In a large skillet melt the butter over medium heat. Add the shallots, mushrooms, bell pepper, almonds, and wild rice. Stir constantly and cook until the almonds are brown, about 20 minutes. Pour the rice mixture into a 1½-quart casserole. In a medium saucepan bring the chicken broth to a boil. Stir the broth into the rice mixture. Cover tightly with aluminum foil and bake for 1½ hours.

The Unidentified Feast

In Jewish tradition there are a number of feasts established by law, as outlined in Leviticus. In writing his Gospel, John often used these specific events to establish the time that something happened. The only unidentified feast mentioned in his book is the one that took place after Jesus healed the nobleman's son. *"After this there was a feast of the Jews, and Jesus went up to Jerusalem"* *[John 5:1]*. So many family memories are holiday-related. Bless your family by celebrating at "unidentified" times.

Marinated Artichoke Salad

Makes 6 servings

dressing

1	tablespoon Dijon mustard
¼	cup tarragon vinegar
½	teaspoon salt
½	teaspoon dried oregano
	pepper, to taste
½	cup corn oil
¼	cup extra-virgin olive oil

salad

8	ounces fresh mushroom slices
1	(14-ounce) can quartered artichoke hearts, drained
1	(14-ounce) can hearts of palm, drained and sliced into ½-inch rounds
24	cherry tomatoes, halved
1	tablespoon capers, drained
6	whole artichokes, trimmed and steamed

For the dressing, combine the mustard and vinegar in a bowl. Add the salt, oregano, and pepper. Whisk in the corn oil and olive oil.

For the salad, place the mushrooms, artichoke hearts, hearts of palm, tomatoes, and capers in a medium bowl. Toss with the dressing, mixing well. Chill overnight.

With a serrated spoon, fill each steamed artichoke with the salad. Pour any remaining dressing over each artichoke and place on a bed of lettuce. Pull the leaves from the artichoke and enjoy.

Romanticism, the artistic movement of the eighteenth
and nineteenth centuries, valued emotion, imagination, and inspiration.
It is often seen as an example of Christianity in its incarnational form. The following words bear testimony:

Ye blessed creatures, I have heard the call
Ye to each other make; I see
The heavens laugh with you in your jubilee;
My heart is at your festival,
My head hath its coronal,
The fullness of your bliss, I feel—I feel it all.
[William Wordsworth, 1770–1850]

Chocolate Toffee Ice Cream Pie

Makes 10 servings

sauce

8	tablespoons (1 stick) butter
1	(11.5-ounce) package chocolate chips
2	cups confectioners' sugar
1	(12-ounce) can evaporated milk
2	teaspoons vanilla extract

pie

12	small Heath bars or 1 (12-ounce) package miniature Heath bars
1	(9-ounce) box chocolate wafers, crushed (about 2 cups)
8	tablespoons (1 stick) butter, melted
½	gallon vanilla ice cream, softened

For the sauce, melt the butter and chocolate chips in a medium saucepan. Add the confectioners' sugar and evaporated milk. Cook over medium heat until thickened, about 15 to 20 minutes, stirring often. Stir in the vanilla and refrigerate until ready to use.

For the pie, place the Heath bars in the freezer to harden. Mix the chocolate wafer crumbs and melted butter together and press on the bottoms and up the sides of two 8-inch pie plates. Place in the freezer to harden.

Remove the Heath bars from the freezer and crush into small pieces. Mix with the ice cream. Fill the pie plates with the ice cream mixture and return to the freezer and freeze overnight.

When ready to serve, heat the sauce and serve over the pie pieces.

"He liveth long who liveth well."
[Horatius Bonar 1809–1889]

Lime Cheesecake with Orange Glaze

Makes 6 to 8 servings

crust

1	cup shortbread cookie crumbs
2	tablespoons butter, melted

filling

24	ounces cream cheese, softened
1	cup sugar
3	eggs
1	tablespoon grated lime zest
¼	cup fresh lime juice

topping

8	ounces fresh strawberries, raspberries, or blueberries
½	cup fresh orange juice
2	teaspoons cornstarch
2	teaspoons sugar

For the crust, combine the cookie crumbs and butter and press into the bottom of a 9-inch springform pan. Refrigerate.

For the filling, preheat the oven to 325 degrees. Beat the cream cheese until smooth. Gradually beat in the sugar. Beat in the eggs, one at a time. Stir in the lime zest and juice until smooth. Pour the mixture into the springform pan and bake 55 to 65 minutes or until set. Turn off the oven and let the cheesecake remain in the oven for 30 minutes with the door slightly open. Remove from the oven and let stand about 10 minutes. Remove the side of the pan and cool on a wire rack. Refrigerate.

For the topping, arrange the berries in a circle on the top of the cooled cheesecake, beginning in the center and working out to the edge of the cheesecake. Bring the orange juice, cornstarch, and sugar to a boil in a small saucepan. Cook for 1 minute. Remove from the heat and let cool a few minutes. Brush the glaze over the top of the cheesecake and chill until time to serve.

Nevertheless He did not leave Himself without witness,
in that He did good, gave us rain from heaven and fruitful seasons, filling our hearts with food and gladness.
[Acts 14:17]

Sunday Roast Chicken

Makes 4 to 6 servings

1	(4-pound) whole roasting chicken
	salt and pepper, to taste
¼	cup balsamic vinegar
1	tablespoon Dijon mustard
2	cloves garlic, minced
2	tablespoons extra-virgin olive oil
2	whole lemons
2	fresh sprigs of rosemary

Wash and pat dry the chicken. Sprinkle with salt and pepper. Combine the vinegar, mustard, garlic, and olive oil in a small bowl. Place the chicken in a large plastic zip-top bag. Pour the marinade over the chicken and seal the bag tightly. Shake the bag to coat the chicken with the marinade. Refrigerate several hours or overnight.

Preheat the oven to 350 degrees. Remove the chicken from the bag and pour off the marinade. Pierce the lemons two or three times with a fork. Place the lemons and the rosemary sprigs into the cavity of the chicken and tie the legs together loosely with kitchen twine. Place breast side down in a roasting pan. Cook for 30 minutes. Turn the chicken over and cook 30 more minutes. Turn the chicken again and raise the temperature to 400 degrees. Roast another 20 to 30 minutes or until the juices run clear. If the top is not brown enough, place the chicken breast side up under the broiler. Let rest a few minutes before carving.

Three Sabbath Gifts

When Isaiah said, "call the Sabbath a delight" [58:13], it was a day of rest, as it was for Jesus when he explained that "the Sabbath was made for man, not man for the Sabbath" [Mark 2:27]. When Acts 20:7 tells us, "Now on the first day of the week," as the disciples came together to break bread, we learn that for us, the Lord's Day had become Sunday, a day for worship. A third, beautiful explanation of the Sabbath is in Hebrews 4:9-10: "There remains therefore a rest for the people of God. For he who has entered His rest has himself also ceased from his works as God did from His." An entirely different Greek word for Sabbath rest is introduced as a foreshadowing of heavenly rest. One word, three gifts. A day of rest, a day of praise and worship, a life eternal.

GiGi's Baked Carrots

Makes 6 to 8 servings

8	carrots, peeled and sliced into rounds (about 4 cups)
4	strips bacon
1	medium onion, finely chopped
	salt and pepper, to taste
¼	cup firmly packed light brown sugar
5	tablespoons butter, melted

Preheat the oven to 400 degrees. Cook the carrots in boiling water in a medium saucepan until tender; drain. Fry the bacon until crisp and remove from pan, reserving the drippings. Sauté the onion in the bacon drippings until tender. Crumble the bacon and add to a 2-quart buttered baking dish. Add the carrots and onion and mix together. Add salt and pepper to taste. Sprinkle the brown sugar over the carrot mixture and pour the melted butter over this. Bake, uncovered, stirring occasionally until the sugar is melted and the carrots are glazed, about 30 minutes.

Homecoming

Family gatherings are often homecomings, the parable of the prodigal son being one of the most well-known homecoming stories in history. When Jesus cured the man possessed by demons, He instructed him to "Go home . . . and tell them what great things the Lord has done for you" [Mark 5:19]. One of the most joyous homecomings of record must have been that of an obscure fourteenth-century traveler named Ibn Battua. For twenty-nine years he traveled throughout Europe and China, covering over seventy-five thousand miles (more than three times the area covered by the renowned traveler Marco Polo). Returning home to Morocco, his words could have been written by most anyone enjoying the blessings of today's prosperity. His "native land was the best of countries, for its fruits are plentiful and running water and nourishing food are never exhausted." Henry van Dyke used a universal voice to pen, "But when it comes to living, there is no place like home." He also wrote the following lesser known lines:

The crown of the home is godliness
The beauty of the home is order
The glory of the home is hospitality
The blessing of the home is contentment

[Henry Van Dyke, 1852–1933]

Cheese Stuffed Zucchini

Makes 6 servings

4	medium zucchini (about 2 pounds)
2	cloves garlic, minced
1	tablespoon tomato paste
1	teaspoon sun-dried tomato bits
½	teaspoon dried oregano
⅓	cup crumbled feta cheese
	salt and pepper, to taste
¼	cup buttery cracker crumbs

Preheat the oven to 350 degrees. Cut the zucchini in half lengthwise and place on a baking sheet. Bake for about 10 minutes to soften; maintain the oven temperature. Remove the zucchini from the oven and scoop out the pulp, leaving the shells intact. Chop the pulp. In a large bowl combine the pulp, garlic, tomato paste, sun-dried tomato bits, oregano, and feta cheese. Season with salt and pepper. Stuff the zucchini shells with the mixture. Sprinkle the cracker crumbs on top of each zucchini and return to the oven for about 10 minutes or until brown and bubbly.

That being made wise, I may conspire to be
As beautiful in thought, and so express
Immortal truths and earth's mortality.
Beauty born of Beauty - that remains.
[Madison Cawein 1865 -1914]

Romaine Salad

Makes 8 to 10 servings

dressing

1	(1¾-ounce) can anchovies
2	cloves garlic, minced
1	tablespoon good quality Dijon mustard (Pommery if possible)
¼	cup red wine vinegar
	salt and pepper, to taste
	juice of ½ lemon
1	cup extra-virgin olive oil

salad

4	hearts of Romaine lettuce, torn into bite-size pieces
	freshly grated Parmigiano-Reggiano cheese
	garlic croutons

For the dressing, mix the anchovies, garlic, mustard, vinegar, salt, pepper, lemon juice, and olive oil in a blender or food processor.

For the salad, combine the lettuce, cheese, and croutons in a serving bowl. Add the dressing to taste and toss to coat.

Fresh Berry Galette

Makes 2 pies, serves 10

3	cups mixed berries, such as blueberries, strawberries, blackberries, or raspberries
1	cup sugar
	juice of 1 lemon
½	teaspoon ground cinnamon
2	(9-inch) rolled refrigerated pie crusts, unfolded
4	tablespoons (½ stick) butter
	vanilla ice cream

Preheat the oven to 375 degrees. In a bowl combine the berries, sugar, lemon juice, and cinnamon. Let stand a few minutes to soften. Place the pie shells on a piece of parchment paper in a large jelly-roll pan. Divide the fruit mixture evenly between each pie shell, 2 inches from the edge of the crust. Fold and pleat the crust over the sides of the fruit mixture. Dot each pie with half the butter. Bake for 25 to 35 minutes, or until the crust is browned and the fruit is cooked. Cut in slices and top with vanilla ice cream.

"Christ, our Passover lamb, was sacrificed for us.
Therefore let us keep the feast, not with old leaven, nor with the leaven of malice and wickedness, but with the
unleavened bread of sincerity and truth" [I Corinthians 5:7-8]. If this beautiful thought remains at the heart of
family gatherings, you may surely exclaim:

The feast is set
The guests are met.
[Samuel Taylor Coleridge, 1772–1834]

And the Fish of the Sea Will Explain to You

[Job 12:8]

Seafood Selections

The immense waters of the world God created are a beautiful declaration and a profound manifestation of His Divine bounty. More species of life dwell within this realm than exist among mammals, reptiles, and birds combined. Based on the letters of the Greek alphabet, *ichthus*, the fish, has from the earliest days of Christianity been a symbol of the faith. Yet its roots can be clearly traced throughout the Old Testament. The state of human helplessness exemplified by the fish in certain passages of scripture is greatly outweighed by the hope and promise of others. In Job 12:8, the title of this chapter, the life contained in the sea is used to explain the natural order of things. Genesis 9:2 "*. . . all the fish of the sea. They are given into your hand*" establishes the power given by God to man. This prosperity is reaffirmed in Isaiah, "*And your heart shall swell with joy; Because the abundance of the sea shall be turned to you*" [60:5]. The seas, rivers, and ponds specifically mentioned in the Old Testament afforded the psalmist a rich source of praise and supplication. "*O Lord, how manifold are Your works! . . . This great and wide sea, In which are innumerable teeming things, Living things both small and great*" [Psalm 104:24–25] is but one example. For Christians, the most relevant Old Testament reference of all is the promise of Ezekiel 47:9–10:

And it shall be that every living thing that moves, wherever the rivers go,
will live There will be a very great multitude of fish, because these waters go there; for they will be healed,
and everything will live wherever the river goes. It shall be that fishermen will stand by it . . .
they will be places for spreading their nets.

The fish as a symbol of Christianity is thus expanded. It becomes an icon, an image, of the premise that in the Testaments of the Holy Bible, the New is concealed in the old, and the Old is revealed in the new.

How natural it seems that in the life of Jesus, many of the most powerful accounts are in a sense "fish stories," from the feeding of thousands to unbelievable catches, on to coins found in a fish's mouth! Following the Crucifixion, the disciples, certainly dazed and overwhelmed, retreated to the sea, to their nets. It was in this familiar setting that Christ appeared to His appointed "fishers of men" for the last time.

But the other disciples came in the little boat . . . dragging the net with fish. Then, as soon as they had come to land, they saw a fire of coals there, and fish laid on it, and bread. Jesus said to them, "Bring some of the fish which you have just caught."

Jesus then came and took the bread and gave it to them, and likewise the fish [John 21:8–10].

This chapter is offered as a visual thanksgiving for the abundant bounty and provision of the sea.

Seafood Selections

Glazed Salmon
with Orange Salsa | 142
Crab and Corn Chowder | 145
Low Country Shrimp
and Sausage Creole | 146
Sage and Smoked Bacon Trout | 149
Oyster and Leek Bisque | 150
Tilapia with Baby Spinach | 155
Crab and Shrimp Casserole | 156
Grilled Tuna | 159
Cajun Snapper Fillets | 160

*These you may eat of all
that are in the water:*
whatever in the water has fins and scales,
whether in the seas or in the rivers—that you may eat.
[Leviticus 11:9]

Glazed Salmon with Orange Salsa

Makes 4 servings

marinade

1	(15-ounce) can Mandarin oranges
2	tablespoons brown sugar
2	tablespoons soy sauce
1	clove garlic, minced
2	teaspoons minced fresh ginger
4	(6-ounce) salmon fillets

orange salsa

1	medium ripe tomato, seeded and chopped
	reserved Mandarin oranges, chopped
1	tablespoon chopped jalapeño chile
¼	cup chopped red bell pepper
1	teaspoon sugar
	salt, to taste

For the marinade, drain the Mandarin oranges, reserving the juice. Set the Mandarin oranges aside to use in the Orange Salsa. In a small bowl, combine the reserved orange juice, the brown sugar, soy sauce, garlic, and ginger. Place the salmon in a shallow dish. Pour the marinade over the salmon and refrigerate for several hours.

For the salsa, in a bowl combine the tomato, Mandarin oranges, jalapeño, bell pepper, sugar, and salt. Refrigerate the salsa until ready to serve.

Preheat a grill to medium. Remove the salmon from the marinade, reserving the marinade. Place skin side down in a grill basket on the grill. Turn the fish after a couple of minutes and baste with the marinade. Continue grilling until the desired degree of doneness. Serve topped with the orange salsa.

I danced for the scribe and the Pharisee
But they would not dance and they would not follow me
I danced for the fishermen, for James and John
They came with me and the dance went on:
Dance, then, wherever you may be,
I am the Lord of the Dance, said he.
[Sydney Carter, 1915–2004]

Taken from "Lord of the Dance" by Sydney Carter

© 1963 Stainer & Bell Ltd. Admin. by Hope Publishing Co., Carol Stream, IL 60188

Crab and Corn Chowder

Makes 4 to 6 servings

3	tablespoons butter, divided
3	green onions, chopped (both stalks and tops)
1	rib celery, chopped
3	ears fresh corn, removed from the cob
1	tablespoon flour
1¼	cups half-and-half
1	cup seafood stock or bottled clam juice
1	(4-ounce) can chopped green chilies, drained
12	ounces lump crabmeat
1	teaspoon Old Bay seasoning

Place 2 tablespoons of the butter in a medium saucepan and sauté the green onions, celery, and corn until tender. Remove 1 cup of this mixture and purée in a blender. Return to the pan.

In a small skillet, melt the remaining 1 tablespoon butter. Stir in the flour and cook about 30 seconds. Stir in the half-and-half and cook until slightly thickened. Add to the corn mixture. Stir in the seafood stock and green chilies. Bring the mixture to a simmer. Carefully stir in the crabmeat and season with the Old Bay seasoning.

"*Joy Is a Net of Love...*"

". . . by which you can catch souls." These words of Agnes Gonxha Bojaxhiu, known to the world as Mother Teresa, are invaluable to Christians as "fishers of men." Although there are three distinct kinds of nets mentioned in the New Testament, the fish are not specified! Is this is an implied permission to witness in whatever way is appropriate?

Again, the kingdom of heaven is like a dragnet that was cast into the sea and gathered some of every kind, which, when it was full, they drew to shore; and they sat down and gathered the good into vessels . . .
[Matthew 13:47–48]

Low Country Shrimp and Sausage Creole

This is a great dish for company. All of the ingredients can be prepared ahead and assembled at the last minute.

Makes 12 to 15 servings

¼	cup vegetable oil
3	cups chopped celery (stalks and leaves)
2	cups chopped mild onion
2	cups chopped green pepper
1	cup raisins, chopped
½	cup chopped fresh parsley
1	(28-ounce) can crushed tomatoes
1	cup chili sauce
1	teaspoon sugar
1	teaspoon dried thyme
1	teaspoon curry powder
3	large bay leaves
	salt and pepper, to taste
3	pounds kielbasa sausage, cut into 3-inch pieces
4	pounds medium shrimp, peeled and deveined
8	to 10 cups cooked white rice
1	cup toasted sliced almonds

In a large stockpot, heat the oil. Add the celery, onion, and green pepper and cook until transparent. Add the raisins, parsley, tomatoes, chili sauce, sugar, thyme, curry powder, bay leaves, salt, and pepper. Simmer, covered, about 30 minutes, or until the sauce is thickened and all the vegetables are tender. Discard the bay leaves.

Cook the sausage on a grill or sauté in a large skillet until browned and cooked through. Keep warm. Bring a large pot of water to a boil. Toss in the shrimp and cook until barely done, about 3 minutes. Drain immediately and set aside.

On a large platter, spread the rice and cover with the almonds. Surround with the cooked sausage. Add the shrimp to the tomato sauce and pour into a large chafing dish. Serve immediately with the rice and sausage.

An Ancient Mariner

Fishermen will go to all lengths for the ultimate catch, but M. Gaius Apicius, a first-century Roman, was certainly among the most extreme. He lived in Campania because of the size of the prawns! Hearing that those in Libya were larger, he set out for that area. Met by a returning fishing boat, he learned they were not as large as reported, so he turned back, never setting foot on African soil. Thinking this to be an antiquated story, fishermen and cooks alike will enjoy knowing that in 1980, the Food and Agriculture Organization of the United Nations published a pamphlet entitled *Catalogue of Shrimps and Prawns of the World*.

Sage and Smoked Bacon Trout

Makes 4 servings

4	(10-ounce) whole rainbow trout, cleaned
	salt and pepper, to taste
12	sprigs of fresh sage
1	pound smoked bacon

Preheat the grill to medium. Season the cavity of the fish with salt and pepper and stuff with 1 sprig of sage. Place 1 large sprig of sage on each side of the fish and wrap the bacon (at least 2 strips) around each fish. Fasten the bacon with wooden toothpicks to secure. Place the fish in a grill basket or individual fish holders. Grill over medium heat about 10 minutes per 1-inch thickness of the fish or until the fish is opaque.

Always have your hook baited,
in the pool you least think, there will be fish.
[Ovid, 43 B.C–A.D. 17]

Oyster and Leek Bisque

Makes 6 to 8 servings

2	ribs celery, chopped
3	small leeks, cleaned and chopped about 2 inches above the white bulb
1	medium onion, chopped
	butter for sautéing
2	(8-ounce) bottles clam juice
½	to ¾ cup half-and-half
2	teaspoons lemon juice
	salt and pepper, to taste
2	pints select oysters

In a medium saucepan sauté the celery, leeks, and onion in butter until soft. Add the clam juice. Cover and simmer about 30 minutes. Purée the mixture in a food processor or blender. Return to the saucepan. When ready to serve, add the half-and-half, lemon juice, salt, and pepper, and oysters. Simmer slowly until the oysters curl. Serve immediately.

We remember the fish which we ate freely in Egypt,
the cucumbers, the melons, the leeks, the onions, and the garlic.
[Numbers 11:5]

"*That light whose smile kindles the universe,*

That beauty in which all things work and move."

[Percy Bysshe Shelley 1792–1882]

Tilapia with Baby Spinach

Makes 2 servings

2	(6-ounce) fresh tilapia fillets
	Everglades Seasoning Salt or your favorite fish seasoning to taste
	flour for dredging
3	tablespoons olive oil, divided
2	cloves garlic, minced
6	ounces baby spinach, rinsed and squeezed dry
½	fresh lemon

Rinse the fish fillets. Sprinkle both sides with seasoning salt and dredge lightly in flour. Heat 2 tablespoons of the oil in a medium skillet. Brown the fish on one side. Turn and cook until opaque. Remove the fillets to a warm plate. Wipe out the skillet and pour in the remaining 1 tablespoon oil. Heat the oil and sauté the garlic about 1 minute. Add the spinach, stirring and cook until just wilted. Divide the spinach between two plates and top with the warm fish. Squeeze fresh lemon juice over all.

. . . we departed and went on our way;
and they all accompanied us, with wives and children, till we were out of the city.
And we knelt down on the shore and prayed.

[Acts 21:5]

Crab and Shrimp Casserole

Makes 10 to 12 servings

1	(6-ounce) package wild and white rice mix (preferably Uncle Ben's)
1	pound sliced fresh mushrooms
8	tablespoons (1 stick) butter, divided
6	tablespoons flour
3½	cups half-and-half
1	tablespoon Worcestershire sauce
	juice of 1 lemon
	salt and pepper, to taste
1	(14-ounce) can artichoke hearts, drained and quartered
2	pounds medium shrimp, peeled and partially cooked
1	pound cooked lump crabmeat
½	cup shredded Parmesan cheese
	paprika for color

Cook the rice mix according to the directions for firmer rice. Set aside.

In a small saucepan sauté the mushrooms in 2 tablespoons of the butter until tender. Set aside. In a medium saucepan heat the remaining 6 tablespoons butter. Add the flour and cook, stirring, for about 1 minute. Remove the pan from the heat and stir in the half-and-half until smooth. Return to the heat and cook, stirring constantly, until lightly thickened. Season with the Worcestershire, lemon juice, salt, and pepper. Taste to adjust the seasonings.

Preheat the oven to 375 degrees. In a 3-quart casserole layer the cooked rice, artichokes, mushrooms, shrimp, and crabmeat. Pour the sauce over the mixture, making sure all of the ingredients are covered. Sprinkle with the Parmesan cheese and paprika. Bake, uncovered, for about 40 minutes or until bubbly and hot in the center.

Those who go down to the sea in ships,
Who do business on great waters,
They see the works of the Lord,
And His wonders in the deep.
[Psalm 107:23–24]

Grilled Tuna

Makes 2 servings

2	tablespoons sesame oil
2	tablespoons soy sauce
¼	cup chopped green onions
2	(¾-pound) sushi-grade tuna steaks, 1-inch thick
	fresh cracked pepper

Combine the oil, soy sauce, and green onions in a shallow dish. Marinate the fish in the dish about 30 minutes.

Heat the grill to medium. Remove the fish from the marinade and grill one side until nicely browned. Turn the fish over, sprinkle with cracked pepper, and cook until the desired degree of doneness.

But while they still did not believe for joy,
and marveled, He said to them, "Have you any food here?"
So they gave Him a piece of a broiled fish and some honeycomb.
And He took it and ate in their presence.
[Luke 24:41–43]

Cajun Snapper Fillets

Makes 4 servings

sauce

1	(14-ounce) can diced tomatoes
1	large sweet onion, chopped
½	cup good quality black olives, such as Kalamata, sliced
8	ounces sliced mushrooms

fish

2	tablespoons olive oil plus more for coating
4	(6 to 8-ounce) red snapper fillets, skinned
	blackened redfish seasoning or other Cajun spice seasoning
2	cloves garlic, minced
	salt and pepper, to taste

For the sauce, in a medium skillet combine the tomatoes, onion, olives, mushrooms, and garlic. Cover and simmer until the onions are tender and the sauce is thickened. Season with salt and pepper. This may be done ahead and re-heated.

For the fish, in a large saucepan heat the oil over medium heat. Rub each side of the fish with a small amount of oil and sprinkle with the redfish seasoning. Rub the minced garlic over the fish and season with salt and pepper. Cook the fish quickly in the hot oil until opaque. Drain on paper towels. Place the fish on a platter and top with the sauce.

A Classical Cook

A fourth-century B.C. Sicilian Greek by the name of Archestratus was most likely the world's first known food writer. His writings were actually in the form of a poem known as the Hedypatheia. He was adamant about using fresh, seasonal produce and as little seasoning as possible. He was wary of the Italians for, "they do not know how to prepare good fish, but wickedly spoil it by putting cheese over everything and dousing it with watery vinegar and pickled silphium." He traveled from Sicily to Byzantium, visiting over fifty places and identifying an equal number of fish. As for dining, he preferred "all to sit at one hospitable table . . . there should be three, or four friends together."

Small Morsels

Kindly to his fellow man;
for dwelling in a house by the side of the road,
he used to entertain all comers.
[Homer, *The Iliad*, Book 6]

Curried Cheese Tart

Makes 3 cups

12	ounces cream cheese, softened
½	pound New York sharp Cheddar cheese, shredded
1	teaspoon curry powder
½	teaspoon salt
1	(8-ounce) jar chutney, drained and chopped
4	green onions, finely chopped (both stalks and tops)

Combine the cream cheese, Cheddar cheese, curry powder, and salt in a bowl. Line a 3-cup tart pan with plastic wrap, extending some of the plastic over the side. Spoon the cheese mixture into the pan, top with more plastic wrap, pressing down until the cheese mixture is evenly spread in the pan. Chill for several hours or overnight. When ready to serve, unmold the cheese and top with the chutney and green onions.

Note: Garnish with red grapes and serve with crackers

. . . both the inner and outer sanctuaries,
with carved figures of cherubim,
palm trees, and open flowers.
[1 Kings 6:29]

If more of us valued food and song
and cheer above hoarded gold, it would be a merrier world.
[J.R.R. Tolkien, 1892–1973]

Dill Sauce for Salmon

Makes 4 cups

2	cups good quality mayonnaise
1	(16-ounce) container sour cream
3	tablespoons minced onion
	Nature's Season Salt, to taste
3	tablespoons chopped fresh dill weed
3	tablespoons chopped fresh parsley
½	peeled, chopped English cucumber, optional

In a large bowl combine the mayonnaise, sour cream, onion, season salt, dill, parsley, and cucumber, if desired. Chill several hours for the flavors to blend. Serve with purchased smoked salmon or fresh vegetables.

Saintly Assistance

Christian brothers cloistered in medieval monasteries are a pleasant, albeit unlikely, source of inspiration for cooks in the midst of preparing beautiful, but labor-intensive items. Consider the words of St. Thomas Aquinas, "The same Spirit who hovered over the waters at the beginning of creation hovers over the mind of the artist at work." Or, call to mind the life of Pascal Baylon, who was designated the patron saint of cooks. His ability to create beautiful and delicious foods, especially bread, from simple ingredients became legendary. St. Francis of Assisi called Christian cheerfulness a study; Francis de Sales termed it a strategy. Let these ideas help you find great happiness as you work with your hands to present "what is good . . . to give" [Ephesians 4:28] to your guests.

Jaiara's Chocolate Truffles

Makes about 16 small balls

2   tablespoons butter
1   (14-ounce) can sweetened condensed milk
3   tablespoons cocoa powder
1   cup chocolate sprinkles

Melt the butter in a nonstick pan over medium heat. Using a long-handled spoon, stir in the sweetened condensed milk and cocoa powder. Cook, stirring constantly, until the mixture starts to bubble and you can see the bottom of the pan. Grease a bowl with butter and pour the mixture into the bowl. Let cool about 30 minutes. Pour the sprinkles into a separate bowl. Roll the cooled chocolate mixture into small balls (a little larger than a teaspoon). Roll the balls in the sprinkles and place on a plate. Refrigerate until ready to serve.

Note: These truffles need to be made in a cool dry kitchen, not on a rainy day.

A Matter of Taste

Flavor, combined with aroma, produces taste. There has always been some disagreement, however, as to how many distinct tastes actually exist. The ancient Chinese believed there to be five: salty, bitter, sour, pungent, and sweet, which correspond to the elements of water, fire, wood, metal, and earth. An eighteenth-century Frenchman started a movement connecting taste to musical notes! Modern gastronomes have proposed adding new tastes, such as the meaty Japanese "umami." When Job wrote, "Does not . . . the mouth taste its food?" [12:11], he could hardly have foreseen that modern, scientific man would disagree as to the exact placement of taste buds in the mouth! Or that, just as a number of people are "color blind," some are also "taste blind." Whatever the facts, the experience of taste is a valid indication that whatever is eaten, even small morsels, should be pleasant.

Cinnamon Crisps

Makes 22 cookies

8	tablespoons (1 stick) butter, softened
1	cup sugar
1	egg
	zest of ½ lemon
2½	cups cake flour, sifted
½	teaspoon baking powder
1	teaspoon cinnamon
½	teaspoon salt
	sugar for sprinkling

Preheat the oven to 350 degrees. Grease a cookie sheet. In a medium mixing bowl, cream the butter and sugar together. Add the egg and continue beating until the mixture is smooth. Add the grated lemon zest. Sift the flour with the baking powder, cinnamon, and salt. Add to the creamed mixture. Divide the dough in half. Roll the dough out thinly onto a surface that has been lightly sprinkled with sugar. Sprinkle the top of the dough with additional sugar. Using cookie cutters, cut the dough into desired shapes and arrange on the prepared cookie sheet. Bake for 15 to 20 minutes.

It's food too fine for angels; yet come, take
And eat thy fill! It's heaven's sugar cake.
[Edward Taylor (c. 1642–1729), Poetical Works, Sacramental Meditations]

To the service of that great and glorious

Being who is the Beneficent Author of all the good that was, that is,

that will be; We unite in rendering unto Him our sincere and humble thanks

for His kind care and protection and for the great degree of tranquility,

union and plenty which we have enjoyed; We most humbly offer . . .

our prayers and supplications to the Great Lord and Ruler of Nations.

[George Washington, 1732–1789]

Blessing to God, forever blest

to God the master of the feast

Who hath for us a table spread

and with his daily bounties fed;

May He with all his gifts impart

The crown of all—a thankful heart.

[Charles Wesley, 1707–1788]

Gratitude is heaven itself.

[William Blake, 1757–1827]

O Lord, You are the portion of my inheritance and my cup;

You maintain my lot. The lines have fallen to me in pleasant places;

Yes, I have a good inheritance . . . You will show me the path of life;

In your presence is fullness of joy;

At Your right hand are pleasures forevermore.

[Psalm 16:5–6, 11]

Oh Lord, that lends me life,
Lend me a heart replete with thankfulness.
[William Shakespeare, 1564–1616]

❧

Let us, with a gladsome mind,
Praise the Lord, for He is kind;
All things living He doth feed,
His full hand supplies their need.
[John Milton, 1608–1674]

❧

Blessed Lord, we pray thee
to be present at our table
hallowing thy gifts to our use;
that eating to satisfy our needs
we may remember those who lack.
[St. Francis of Assisi, c. 1181–1226]

May God be praised
that all things be so good.
[John Donne, 1572–1631]

❧

Oh my God,
for providing senses to enjoy delights,
for thy royal bounty providing my daily support,
for a full table and overflowing cup,
for appetite, taste, sweetness,
for social joys of relatives and friends
for opportunities of spreading happiness around,
for loved ones in the joys of heaven,
I love thee above the powers of language to express,
For what thou art to thy creatures. Amen.
[17th-century Puritan meditation]

Reprinted with permission from Banner of Truth Trust, P.O. Box 621, Carlisle, PA 17013.

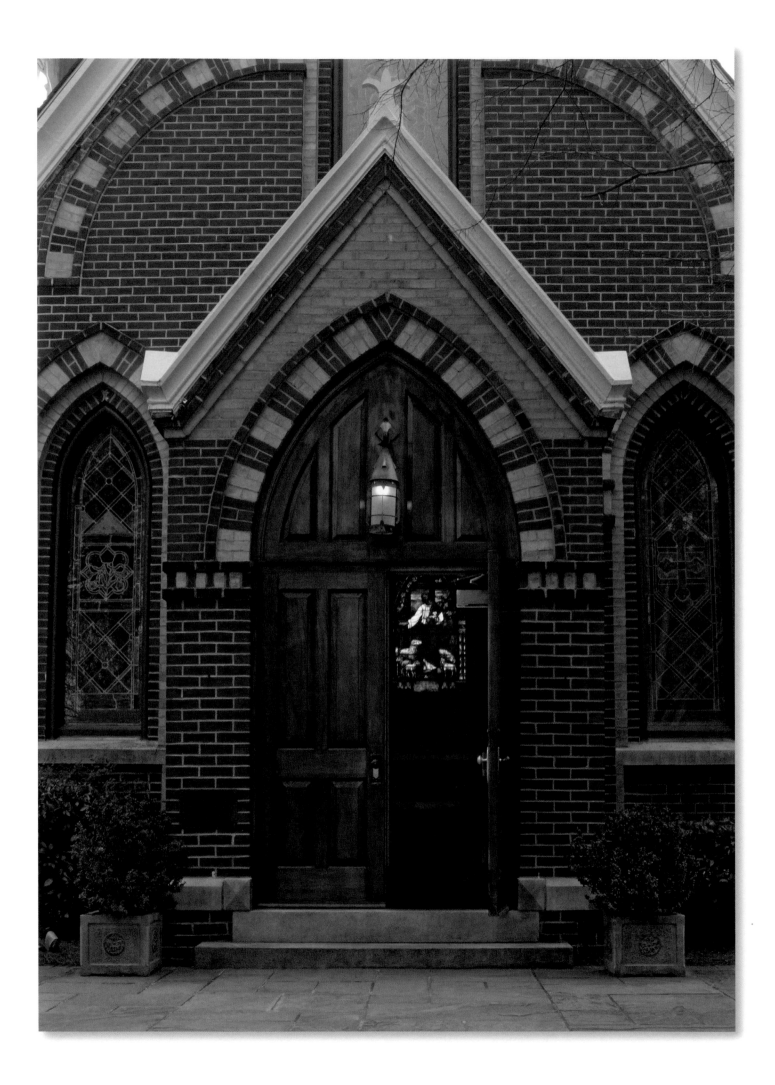

Grace Be With You
[Colossians 4:18]

A Valediction

God intends for us, as sacred life travelers, to celebrate and enjoy His bounty. Jesus said, "I have come that they may have life, and that they may have it more abundantly" [John 10:10]. His yearning is that we enjoy life, that it be full and meaningful. God's desire is for all humanity to partake of the bounty He created. This celebration of life was intended by God to be a way of life now and as preparation for a future event in which, as followers of Christ, all are invited to participate. A banquet that will cause all other banquets to pale in comparison, "Eye has not seen, nor ear heard, Nor have entered into the heart of man The things which God has prepared for those who loved Him" [1 Corinthians 2:9], is the marriage supper of the Lamb. Jesus exhibited this commitment to joyous celebration by performing His first miracle at the wedding in Cana of Galilee. When He changed the water into wine, the host said to the bridegroom, you have saved the best for last. This, dear friends, is a prophetic reminder that our God has also saved the best not only for last but forever. In our limited ability, we have tried to portray with beauty and creativity the beautiful bounty of God's provision. We humbly acknowledge that we have only scratched the surface of what God desires and plans for us to enjoy for all eternity.

—Steve Wingfield

"If anyone hears My voice and opens the door,
I will come in to him and dine with him, and he with Me"
[Revelation 3:20]

Not That We Are
Sufficient of Ourselves
[2 Corinthians 3:5]

Acknowledgments

The collaborators of Come to the Table would like to thank the following people for their assistance. The cheerfulness with which you offered your help was a gift in itself.

Mr. John B. Long
Dr. John C. Mitchell (in memoriam)
Mr. James T. Wilson, Jr

DESIGN IMAGES AND GIFTS
Mrs. Jenny Addie
The Honorable and Mrs H. Scott Allen
Mrs. Maryann Mell Baggs
Mrs.Thomas W. Blanchard
Mr. and Mrs. R. Daniel Blanton
Mr. and Mrs. G. Waring Boys
Mr. and Mrs. Michael Brown
Charleston Street Florist
Mr. Albert F. Cheatham
Mrs. Larry Coggins
Church of the Good Shepherd
Mr. and Mrs. Edwin L. Douglass, Jr.
Mr. and Mrs. W. Stewart Flanagin, Jr.
Georgia State Floral Distributors
Dr. and Mrs. H. North Goodwin

Dr. Henry N. Goodwin, Jr.
Mrs. Joseph Hart
Mrs. Alonzo Key
Mr. and Mrs. Boone A. Knox
Mr. and Mrs. Samuel F. Maguire
Mrs. James Hampton Manning, Jr.
Mr. and Mrs. John S. Markwalter
Mr. and Mrs. Finley H. Merry
Dr. and Mrs.Logan Nalley, Jr.
Mr. and Mrs. J. Haley Roberts, Jr.
Simply Kitchens
Mrs. Thomas Swift
Dr. and Mrs. George W. Thurmond
Mr. and Mrs Raworth Williamson
Mr. and Mrs. James T. Wilson, III

We are especially grateful to our constant and faithful friends at Thomas Nelson: Pamela Clements, Randy Elliott, and of course our most patient editor, Geoffrey Stone, who with dauntless courage led three steel magnolias through the intricacies of the publishing world. Without your support this project would never have come to fruition.

We thank you all, and know that "... you will be blessed"
[Luke 14:14]

Index

Recipes and Names